UNDERSTANDING PERCEPTION

Understanding Perception

The Concept and its Conditions

D.W. HAMLYN

Avebury

Aldershot · Brookfield USA · Hong Kong · Singapore · Sydney

Published by
Avebury
Ashgate Publishing Ltd
Gower House
Croft Road
Aldershot
Hants GU11 3HR
England

Ashgate Publishing Company
Old Post Road
Brookfield
Vermont 05036
USA

British Library Cataloguing in Publication Data

Hamlyn, D.W. (David Walter)
    Understanding perception : the concept and its conditions
    1. Perception 2. Perception (Philosophy)
    1. Title
    121. 3

    ISBN 1 85972 375 6

Library of Congress Catalogue Card Number: 96-83218

Printed in Great Britain by Antony Rowe Ltd,
Chippenham, Wiltshire

Contents

Preface

This book is meant to sum up my thinking about perception, which began at least as early as my first book, *The Psychology of Perception*, which was published in 1957. In that sense it is a product of something like a life-time of thinking about the subject. Its form owes something to a seminar on perception which I gave shortly before I retired from the Chair of Philosophy at Birkbeck College in 1988. But its content is far from being restricted to what went on then. Nevertheless, I should like to acknowledge yet again what I owe to colleagues and students at Birkbeck College, particularly the latter, if I can say so without meaning to give offence to the former. There are others to whom I owe much for urging me to write this book. There are two in particular, who happen to be old students of mine, James Bennett, and Chris Olsen of OISE in Toronto. Finally there is my wife, Eileen, to whom I owe so much in many ways. Apart from anything else, she has read the typescript and corrected many errors, while making encouraging noises. But that is just the beginning of it.

I would like to dedicate this book to my grand-daughter, Sarah, reference to whom is made in a note to chapter 10.

Chapter 1
What is a theory of perception?

A theory of X should explain, to one extent or another, matters which fall within the domain of X. A theory of perception should therefore explain, in some way, matters which fall under the heading of perception. Unfortunately, that does very little to make clear what one should write about if one is to set out a theory of perception. The subject of perception is one which, traditionally, has fallen across a number of disciplines, and is likely to continue to do so, as consideration of a simple model will make clear. Suppose that one considers the simple, and in many ways unreal, example of someone looking at, and therefore seeing, an object – say a candle. That candle, if lit, will emit light of a certain kind and with a certain pattern, so that light rays, conforming to some extent to that pattern, pass to the eyes of the person in question, through the lenses which the eyes contain. What happens up to that point is the concern of physics, and an investigation of what happens falls within the domain of physical optics, although at the back of that will be matters which can be thought of from a purely geometrical point of view and therefore belong to geometrical optics.

What happens within the body of the person concerned once the eyes are stimulated by the light emitted by the candle is a matter for physiology. This will involve not only what happens at the level of the retina, but what happens in the optical tracts and then in the brain. It has seemed natural to many to suppose that all that is then left out is the final perceptual experience, which can then be left to psychology. But psychologists are concerned with much more than that, including the question how everything that has been mentioned up to this point can be thought to provide us with information about the candle, and why the candle looks as it does in these circumstances. Part of this has to do with the functions that perception performs. If, for example, one regards the function of perception as making possible information pick-up, then there are obvious questions about how this works and what considerations make it possible. The psychologist J.J. Gibson has called this 'ecological optics' [1] since the questions involve considerations about the relation of the perceiver to his or her ecological environment. Gibson thought that the psychology of perception could thus be simply a matter of what in the stimulus array makes possible the pick-up of information about the world.

Other psychologists, while recognising Gibson's contributions to the subject, have thought it incredible that it should be suggested that nothing more needs to be said about the mechanisms in us which make information pick-up possible. One need not suppose that those mechanisms can be left to the physiologist, since we may want to know, not the nature and composition of those mechanisms, but their functional role or roles. One supposition might be that their role is computational;2 they compute on the basis of what is fed into the senses (in the way that information, so-called, is fed into a computer) what is to be learnt about the source of the stimulation. Whether that is how it actually is need not be our concern now; all that needs to be brought out is that there are genuine questions about the functional roles that sense-organs and elements of them and their physiological backing have to perform in enabling us, by means of perception, to gain information about the world.

But perception's role is not merely to provide us with information about the world, so enabling us to have beliefs, and indeed knowledge, about the world. How that candle looks to the person concerned may be an aesthetic matter as well as a purely intellectual matter of the information provided about it. If that seems too strong a way of putting what is involved in quite ordinary seeing, it nevertheless seems on the face of it that there is more to the look of a thing than being given information of what it is or is like. That is a point to which I shall return, but, in any case, there is nothing in a story about information pick-up which seems to say anything about the perceptual *experience* itself, something that has seemed to many traditional thinkers about perception to be the crucial element in perception, and the end-product of the processes studied, as noted, by those from other disciplines. What is the relation of that experience to the information pick-up? Does it contribute in a significant way to the performance of the functional roles involved? These are clearly questions which a theory of perception ought to include. Other such questions will be ones about the contribution, if any, made by other elements of our psychology, by, for example, the concepts, beliefs, feelings, aims and intentions which we have.

I have not so far mentioned anything specifically about philosophy, nor said anything about what a philosophical theory of perception might be. One answer to the question what it might be is possibly that it is illustrated by what I have been saying up to this point. That is to say that at any rate one philosophical exercise about perception is to set out the various components in thinking about perception and to try to explain how they all fit together – or at least to make clear the questions about that which are at issue. Something like that approach is to be found in Aristotle's discussion of perception (*aisthêsis*) in his *De Anima*. There Aristotle starts from what he takes to be the obvious position – one adopted widely by his predecessors – that perception is a form of being affected. This is to say that in perception something about us, our senses or, more specifically, our sense-organs is affected by the objects which we perceive. It cannot be just that, however, since a sense-organ, like any other object, could be affected, in the sense that it could be changed, by the influence of another object without that amounting to perception. Today we might be inclined to say that for the change to constitute perception it must at least be the case that it sets up some experience in us; but Aristotle does not say that and it is not clear that there is any way in which he could have said that clearly by means of any words available in ancient Greek. Instead, he puts refinements on the story about being affected, saying that the object of perception actualises a potentiality already in the sense-organ so as to become like that object in some way. An alternative formula used to that end is that in sense-perception the sense (by which he means, on the most plausible interpretation, the sense-organ) receives the form of the object without its matter. It does this, however, only if some other conditions are satisfied, particularly that there must be a medium and that there is an appropriate relation (what he calls a 'mean') between the condition of the object and that of the sense-organ.

It may seem that Aristotle's account is too physiological to be classified as of the kind that I mentioned above – one which tries to fit together the various components in our thinking about perception. It is true that the account is largely biologically inspired, and that puts limits on its philosophical utility. But Aristotle also sees it as necessary to speak of perception involving judgment or at least discrimination. Judgment is discursive and involves concepts, so that there is a link between perception and thought, a potentiality for which must be supposed to be exercised when a sense-organ is stimulated. I do not suggest that Aristotle is at all clear about how these different elements fall together, but it *is* clear that he recognises the necessity of introducing refinements on the purely causal accounts offered by his Presocratic predecessors, particularly the Atomists whose account was not only purely causal but also purely physical. Elsewhere in Aristotle's works there are to be found other pertinent observations about perception. It is arguable whether there is to be found anything about perception as a form of consciousness, but there is certainly nothing about perceptual experience. In the *De Anima* Aristotle's account can be characterised as an attempt to set out the conditions which are both necessary and sufficient for perception of an object to occur. One might say that he is trying to set out a theory of the form 'It is true to say that X perceives object M if and only if ...', where what follows the 'if and only if' constitutes a set of refinements on a physical/biological relation between object and sense-organ. We shall see later that there may be other projects having a similar form but with different presuppositions.

Descartes thought that the supposition that in perception the form or species is passed into the mind was nonsense. In his *Dioptric*, I, he said that visual perception is like the use of a stick by a blind man. What are communicated to the brain are simply movements. These set up ideas in the mind, but there is no question of the form of the object being passed on by any mechanism. So he was out of sympathy with the kind of approach to perception that Aristotle adopted, and even more, perhaps, out of sympathy with the approach of Aristotle's successors in the Middle

Ages, particularly Aquinas, who saw it all as an account of how objects affect the *mind*. The Cartesian 'way of ideas', combined with the view that such ideas are that of which we have direct awareness and are at best representational of objects 'outside the mind', led to a conception of the nature of philosophical theories of perception quite different from any which we have considered so far. That conception was largely epistemologically inspired, which Aristotle's theory was not, and which the kind of philosophical approach which I have so far mentioned is also not.

I do not say that no theory of perception presented before this time was epistemological in character. Certainly Plato, for example, was concerned with the question whether perception provided knowledge; for at any rate most of his philosophical life, he was inclined, because of his rather special conception of knowledge, to say that perception did not provide knowledge. This, however, was not because perception involved any special objects other than quite ordinary things; it was because the objects of *knowledge* were special, his so-called Forms. By contrast, for Descartes and those philosophers who followed him, the objects of perception were ideas, sensations, impressions or whatever terminology seemed suitable for picking out the immediate objects of the senses. At best such objects of perception were representational of the objects which existed 'outside the mind'; at worst, if that is the right way to put it, such objects were the only 'real things', as with Berkeley's idealism. A theory of perception in these terms was a theory which spelled out the relations which existed, if any did, between ideas or representations of perception and things in the physical world. Moreover, that physical world was thought to be 'external', since it was supposed that we are initially confined epistemologically to those things, such as ideas, which are within the mind, with the result that the world in which we live is inevitably external to us, being external to the mind, and not merely external to our bodies. This 'Cartesian' legacy has had a long history, elements of which I shall return to later.

Given all this, there is a supposed problem about our knowledge of the 'external world' and about the part which perception plays in this. If it is supposed that our ideas are in some way representations of physical things, how can we know this? Are such representations caused by physical things, and if so by what kind of causal link, and how again can we know about it if our perception is immediately confined to such representations? On the other hand, if the impossibility of such knowledge makes the whole conception of a representational relation itself impossible or incredible, are we left with idealism, the thesis that reality consists in some way only of ideas? Or can we safeguard the reality of physical things while making them, as it has been put, logical constructions out of ideas, in accordance with what has become known as phenomenalism, in terms of which, while there are both physical things and ideas, sensations or sense-data, what we understand by the former has to be explicated in some way in terms of the latter?

One curiosity about such epistemological theories of perception – the representative theory, the causal theory, phenomenalism, and so on – is that their proponents paid comparatively little attention to the question what perception actually is, in the way in which, as we have seen, Aristotle did, whatever one thinks of his account. There tended to be the assumption that perception was just something like sensation, although the connection between perception and the beliefs which were, supposedly, founded on it meant that something like judgment had to enter the picture somewhere. Thomas Reid, who in the 18th century, found Hume's philosophy unsatisfactory and thought that the trouble lay in the premises of his argument – in what Hume had to say about impressions and ideas – made a sharp contrast between sensation and perception. Sensation, he said, was an act of mind which has no object other than itself. Perception, by contrast, was directed to objects in the world, and involved concepts of such objects, together with beliefs in their existence which were not the result of any reasoning or inference. Sensations, he said, may 'suggest' such perceptions to us. Whatever one thinks of the details of this, the account clearly involves an attempt to grapple with the concept of perception, to make clear what perception is. Although subsequent philosophers for long paid little attention to Reid or to such an account, what Reid had to say is clearly something that might be called a philosophical theory of perception.

Someone might object that it is not clear why it is not psychology, since the account makes reference to various aspects of the mind's workings. A short answer is that it is philosophical because it provides some kind of analysis of what we mean by 'perception'; the inquiry is a conceptual one. What then would distinguish a *psychological* theory of perception? When I wrote my *The Psychology of Perception* in 1957,[3] I took as my point of departure in trying to answer that question a further question considered by the Gestalt psychologist, Kurt Koffka, in his *Principles of Gestalt Psychology*,[4] 'Why do things look as they do?' For present purposes, Koffka's own answer to that question does not matter, although it is of some importance that he thought that a single answer to it was possible. By contrast, I argued that it mattered whether one was concerned with things looking right or looking wrong, with whether one's concern is with veridical perception or with illusions. The question 'Why?' might be answered differently depending on whether the concern was with veridical perception on the assumption that one might be expected not to get things right or whether the concern was with illusions on the opposite assumption. (I considered a third possibility, but that need not be our concern now.) The crucial point is that 'perception' is not the name of some process which is neutral in respect of being right or wrong; the possibility of being right or wrong is endemic to whatever falls under that concept. At all events, psychology might be concerned to explain various perceptual illusions to which we may be subject and, though differently, to explain why we sometimes manage to see things aright when we might be expected not to. Whatever may be said about the details of that thesis, psychologists have certainly been concerned with the explanation of illusions and the explanation of our success in seeing things as more or less the right size, shape and colour despite apparently unfavourable circumstances, as with the so-called 'perceptual constancies' (where things look as of more or less constant size, shape and colour despite variation in the conditions of perception).

Jerry Fodor pointed out in his first book, *Psychological Explanation* ,5 that psychologists might be concerned with a further question – not just *why* we perceive things in the way that we do, but *how* we perceive them in these ways. This is fair comment, although the question 'How do we perceive things?' is ambiguous as it stands in that it might mean (a) what is it in human beings that makes perception possible?, or (b) how do people manage to see things? The former question might be a response to scepticism about the very possibility of perception and that is not obviously a matter for psychology. The latter question is presumably a request to be told how perception works, what mechanisms or functions bring perception about. Even so, it is answerable at different levels. It may be a request to be told about the relative parts played in perception by such things as sensation, concepts and judgment; it may, by contrast, be a request to be told about the 'mechanisms of perception' or at least about the functions that putative mechanisms have to play. In that spirit J.J. Gibson can be taken to have said that we perceive things through the senses, considered as perceptual systems, picking up information from the stimulus-array, although he also claimed that it was not necessary to say anything more about any additional mechanisms or functions that have to be performed in order to make information pick-up possible. By contrast David Marr can be taken to have said that we need also to know about the principles of computation that are used in information pick-up, although the realisation of those principles in actual physiological mechanisms is another matter, and not one specifically for psychology.

It might be asked, however, why one should not to this end make reference to such things as sensory experience, concepts and judgments. To do so would be to go beyond treating the senses simply as perceptual *systems*, whatever the functions of those systems are supposed to be. It is clear, for example, that to treat the senses as systems concerned simply with information pick-up is to suppose that perception is no more than information pick-up; the view necessarily avoids reference to any of the experiential aspects of perception. The same is not obviously true in quite the same way of a refusal to have anything to do with such things as concepts and judgments in an account of perception. Whether they need to be brought into a theory of information pick-up depends on exactly what is meant by 'information' in this context. If, as Gibson claims,6 the sense of 'information' that he is concerned with is that of 'information about' and not, as he puts it, information in the sense of structure, that suggests that he is concerned with something like the ordinary sense of 'information'. In that case information pick-up would presuppose understanding and therefore concepts on the part of the person involved and it would follow that the senses cannot in this context be treated as systems the function of which is independent of everything else about the person whose senses they are. On the other hand, if the sense of 'information' involved is that employed by those concerned with information processing in the technical and possibly computational sense, the situation is quite different, but the question that then arises is whether an account built on this sense of 'information' does justice to the very notion of perception. And that is a philosophical question.

It is a philosophical question because it presupposes a general understanding of what perception amounts to and how it fits in with the other things that go to make up the mind, just as an epistemological theory of perception in the sense which I noted earlier attempts to set out the part played by perception in relation to knowledge. It is a philosophical theory of perception in so far as it contributes to the philosophy of mind. A psychologist might conceivably ask what role is played by, say, concepts in enabling us to see certain things in certain sorts of ways (although contemporary psychologists, as contributors to cognitive psychology, do not generally or characteristically ask such questions), but that perception involves concepts, to the extent that it does, is a philosophical matter because it involves an appeal to an understanding of the concept of perception which is, at best, presupposed by psychologists.

How much, however, does that understanding, the understanding of the concept of perception, presuppose in the way of knowledge of the details of the processes which make perception possible? It has sometimes been claimed that no knowledge of such details is necessary, on the grounds that we all know perfectly well what it is to perceive things, without needing to know any of the technical details of what makes perception possible. Moreover, the early Greeks, for example, knew perfectly well how to speak of perception and in that sense knew quite well what it is to perceive things, while getting at least some of the details of the processes which make perception possible quite wrong. But there would surely be something very odd if they got the details of those processes entirely wrong. Moreover, it should not be presumed that our common-sense understanding of what is involved could not be corrected at certain points by scientists with greater knowledge of what is involved. What one needs is what is sufficient for answering the question whether some being can perceive, and for that purpose one needs at least a working knowledge of the kinds of processes involved, but not necessarily knowledge of all the details. What such a working knowledge amounts to cannot be answered in a general way; it depends on the particular questions being asked. For philosophical success in this area, as elsewhere, a sense of the appropriate questions and about what they really amount to is sometimes as important as providing the answers to them.

But one thing is clear – that in trying to provide an understanding of perception it is not enough simply to list the components involved in it – causal processes, sensations, concepts and so on. One needs to know how they fit together. One of the big issues in this area, for example, is how the experiences one has are related to one's belief and knowledge about the world. Another is how the causal processes involved are to be seen as related to the ways in which things look to us, and what indeed it is for things to look such and such to us. All such matters are ones on which a philosophical theory of perception ought to cast light.

Notes

1 See Gibson, J.J., *The Senses Considered as Perceptual Systems*, Houghton Mifflin: Boston, Mass., (1966) and Routledge and Kegan Paul: London, (1968); (1979), *The Ecological Approach to Visual Perception*, Houghton Mifflin: Boston, Mass.

2 See particularly Marr, D. (1982), *Vision*, W.H.Freeman: San Francisco. Marr is well known for setting out a three-level account of perception. Level one is concerned with the function involved, although Marr expresses that in computational terms so that level two is said to be concerned with the appropriate algorithm for fulfilling that function; it is really concerned with the precise implementation of the function. Level three is concerned with the physical realisation of it all.

3 Hamlyn, D.W. (1957), *The Psychology of Perception*, Routledge and Kegan Paul: London; reprinted with new appendix in 1969.

4 Koffka, K. (1935), *Principles of Gestalt Psychology*, Routledge and Kegan Paul: London.

5 Fodor, Jerry A. (1968), *Psychological Explanation*, Random House: New York.

6 Gibson, op. cit., p.245.

Chapter 2
Perceptual data

Forty or fifty years ago the philosophy of perception, at least as practised within Anglo-Saxon philosophy, was largely devoted to a consideration of so-called sense-data and of their relation to so-called material or physical objects. I speak of these things as 'so-called' because the terms involved are all terms of art. It will not do to say that by material or physical objects is meant simply objects of perception in the world, first because those who espoused sense-data sometimes claimed that it was these which were the objects of perception, or at any rate, direct objects of perception, and were in the world or were not merely subjective (though that belief was not uniform among exponents of the notion); second because some of the things in the world which we perceive may not be material or physical in a literal sense (whatever that is). By the latter I do not mean to invoke the ideas of seeing ghosts, for example, though the phrase 'seeing ghosts' is a quite accepted one; I have in mind the fact that we sometimes perceive pictures, cinema and television images and so on, and while these all have a material and physical basis they are not in themselves just material or physical objects. (There is also the fact that we perceive facts, we perceive that such and such is the case, but whether these constitute *objects* of perception is arguable.) It has indeed been claimed that the term 'material object' gets its sense in the discussions of perception which I am at present concerned with only by contrast with the term 'sense-datum'. Whether or not that is the case, one needs to raise the question whether there are such things as sense-data.

This was for long a question which was not even asked; that there were sense-data was taken for granted by philosophers. It has been said that the *term* was introduced into philosophy only comparatively recently in this century, by perhaps G.E. Moore; but, as has equally been pointed out, the *idea* goes back much further. It found expression in what earlier philosophers, such as Berkeley, said about sensations and ideas, what Hume said about impressions of sense, and what Kant and other German philosophers said about representations (*Vorstellungen* – better

9

perhaps presentations, presentations to the mind, although they were often thought to be representations of things in reality). There is even something like the idea to be found in what Plato says about knowledge not lying in our impressions (or experiences – *pathêmata*, ways of being affected), although what he says may not have all the implications that later philosophers read into impressions, sensations, sense-data and the like.

I make this last point because, while it is common to all philosophers employing these notions that in perception we are affected in some way, it is a more refined idea, affected by epistemological considerations, that in being so affected we are provided with a datum, a given, which has some kind of certainty as far as experience is concerned. Aristotle's account of perception in his *De Anima*, for example, amounts to a series of refinements on the idea that perception is a form of being affected (a conception that he finds in his Presocratic predecessors), but which needs to be refined, if perception, as a form of being affected, is to be distinguished from other ways in which changes can be brought about in us, and in our sense-organs in particular, by objects outside our bodies. Thus he suggests, as noted in chapter 1, that in perception objects actualise a potentiality in sense-organs to become like those objects, or that the sense (meaning almost certainly the sense-organ) receives the form of the object without its matter, provided that there is a medium and a proportionate relation between the states of the object and the sense-organ. But if all these constitute ways of being affected (something which at one point at least, 431a5, Aristotle qualifies to the extent of rejecting the idea) there is no tendency on Aristotle's part to suggest that perceptual experience consists ultimately of items of given information – data in that sense. But that is exactly how it is with Berkeleian sensations and Humean impressions. Moreover, in the case of those latter philosophers, if what is given in those sensations and impressions is to be truly a datum, and provide the certain foundation for the rest of knowledge, the given information must ultimately be simple or atomic, so that the knowledge based on such things can arise from complication or elaboration of what is thus simple.

In that way, the data of sense are not merely given to us by the affection of our senses; they constitute 'givens' in themselves, providing epistemological foundations for the rest of our experience, our beliefs and indeed our knowledge. A student once said to me 'Surely something must be given in experience'. If that means that there are items of information which we are provided with by the ways in which our senses are affected, well and good; if it means that those items of information constitute epistemological 'givens' in the sense which I have tried to indicate, that is quite another matter. That idea has in any case not gone without criticism even among philosophers who might be thought to belong to the tradition established by Descartes, which was concerned with the search for certainty. Malebranche, for example, said that some sensations were really a species of judgment, which he called natural judgments or judgments of sense, as opposed to free judgments. Moreover, at a later time and in a somewhat different tradition, Hegel, followed by other Hegelians such as Bradley, argued that there could not be anything in experience which was immediate, not mediated by judgment (apart, perhaps, from the bare fact that it is experience), because in so far as what was experienced had content it had to be mediated by concepts, which implied judgment.

This, Hegel thought, applied even to the thought that something is a 'this', 'now' or 'me' (i.e. an 'I'). Bradley followed him in this, claiming that 'this' for example indicated a position in a series. Both philosophers, therefore, thought that these terms were as universal or general in character as other more obviously general terms; the terms in question were similarly applicable to a number of instances, though that is not enough in itself to clinch the argument. Indexicals, of which these terms are examples, may presuppose in their use appeal to considerations of a general sort, but that does not override the differences in their logical role from that of predicative terms such as 'red'. Nevertheless, the issue is not without importance when one comes to the question what content the 'given' can be thought to have, while remaining a given and thus being beyond argument, or, as it came to be put by some sense-datum philosophers, incorrigible. Both Russell and Ayer came to suggest at times that the only adequate examples of sense-data statements, i.e. statements the expression of which in sentences has a content which can properly characterise what is given in sense perception, would be statements like 'Red here now'. It was thought that this kind of sentence was as near as possible to one containing only indexicals (it being presumed that 'red' in this use is not an ordinary predicative expression, whatever it is). If the Hegelians were right, this thought is misconceived, and even if they were not right in their reasons for holding what they did about indexicals, it remains difficult to see what characterisation of experience could be unmediated by some general consideration, that is to say by concepts. If so, we are never given information in perception which has a certainty or incorrigibility about it which is independent of thought or judgment, and which could thus play the epistemological role of providing a foundation for the rest of knowledge.

In spite of this, philosophers in the tradition of 20th century empiricism who have defended recourse to the idea of sense-data have generally done so in one of two ways. The first approach, which might be described as the phenomenological one, has been to appeal to certain examples of experiences in which it is supposedly clear that something is directly present to consciousness or is directly apprehended.[1] Apart from any questions which might be raised about the examples, the notions of being directly present to consciousness or being directly apprehended are open to objections of the kind that Hegel brought to bear on the idea that there are forms of consciousness which are unmediated by concepts. To the extent that what is presented to consciousness or is apprehended has content, to that extent it can be argued that there is nothing direct about it, in the sense that in the experience we are simply given something, some information, which implies no recourse to anything else.

The second approach, invoked, for example, by Ayer,[2] is to suggest that if one progressively reduces one's claims about what one is perceiving one will eventually arrive at a bottom-level claim about what appears to one, an absolute, so to speak.

If one puts the issue in that way, it must be evident that it is just an assumption that there is a final term to the progression involved in so reducing one's claims about what one perceives. Alternatively, if it is agreed, simply for the sake of argument, that there is such a final term, it is far from clear that the final claim can be put in terms of something appearing to one such and such. Ayer in fact moves from 'It now seems to me that I see a cigarette case' to 'I am now seeing a seeming-cigarette case', and claims that the seeming-cigarette case is an example of a sense-datum. This move in fact attracted considerable adverse comment, but the question remains in any case why it should be supposed that the suggested sense-datum claim is a bottom-level claim. It might simply be a technical way, perhaps a not altogether attractive way, of trying to characterise one's experience without commitment to any claim about what actually exists independently of one's perception. Indeed, earlier in his *Foundations of Empirical Knowledge*, Ayer had claimed that the point of reference to sense-data was one simply of convenience in enabling one to 'refer to the contents of our sense-experiences, without referring to material things'.3 But this suggests only that talk of sense-data is simply a convenient way of describing perceptual experiences, and in that case the questions arise what exactly is meant by 'perceptual experiences' here and what on earth is convenient about the usage. Other philosophers have come to invoke the term 'sense-datum' as a kind of technical term, a shorthand device for describing the situations in which it appears to us that such and such. H.P. Grice did this, for example, in an influential paper on the causal theory of perception,4 which I shall consider in chapter 4. Grice argued that there were neutral uses of 'it appears that', without any such presuppositions as that the there was doubt whether the object was in fact as it appeared or that it was implied that it was not in fact as it appeared. The notion of a sense-datum could be invoked, therefore, as a short-hand device for referring to such appearances and some kind of theory of perception could then be built on such a notion of sense-data. Whether or not that is justified need not be considered at the moment; but it ought to be clear that neither the notion of sense-data invoked here nor the resulting theory is directly epistemological in character, in the sense of seeking to find a foundation for knowledge in perceptual experience. The situation was different with the earlier sense-datum philosophers.

What those who have appealed to a notion like that of direct apprehension have been concerned with might be described as sensory intuitions or what Russell called 'knowledge by acquaintance'.5 Russell held that such knowledge by acquaintance was quite different from knowledge of truths and involved no such knowledge of truths. It thus involved an appeal to something that the Idealists, such as Bradley, thought quite impossible, at any rate at the level of sense-experience. Knowledge by acquaintance was, however, opposed directly to another form of knowledge of objects, knowledge by description, in which descriptions applicable to objects, and thus concepts under which they could be brought, were invoked. Knowledge by description is different from knowledge of truths, being, as I have said, a form of knowledge of objects, but it obviously presupposes knowledge of truths or at any rate knowledge of the applicability of descriptions to objects. Hegel and the

Idealists would thus have said, quite rightly, that such knowledge, although of objects, is a form of knowledge which is mediated and not immediate. Knowledge by acquaintance, on the other hand, is not the same as the ordinary notion of acquaintance, in terms of which we may be acquainted with, say, a person, knowing things about him in consequence. It is supposed to be something quite immediate, involving in itself no knowledge *about* its object, however much it may make such knowledge about the object possible. But that idea, that of a form of knowledge of objects which has no propositionally expressible content seems incoherent. Hence the subsequent attempts to find some minimal propositional form which could be said to characterise sense-data while still maintaining the immediacy which knowledge of sense-data was supposed to have. It is a lost cause.

It might be objected that the Idealist position, which I am implicitly supporting, implies that there is nothing below the level of judgment and that, if this is so, the question arises what distinguishes perceptual judgments from other judgments. If that question is to be answered by appeal to other, non-judgmental, elements in perception, such as, perhaps, sensations, that simply provokes other questions about how it all fits together. I shall come to such questions later, but it might be as well to note now that more recently there have been other attempts to mark off judgment or belief (which involve concept-use) from perception by arguing that, unlike judgment or belief, perception has a content which is, wholly or partly, non-conceptual. One of the earliest examples of this trend is to be found in Gareth Evans' *The Varieties of Reference*, chapter 5.6 Evans notes there (p.121) that what he has in mind is the idea of a perceiver being an information-receiving system, in the sense of 'information' which is involved in theories of information-processing put forward in the context of cognitive science (although he also refers, to my mind mistakenly, to the work of J.J. Gibson in this connection). He says, however, that 'a traditional epistemologist would have recast these platitudes in terms of the concepts of *sensation* and *belief*, where by 'sensation' he has in mind sense-data or their equivalent. This suggests that the idea of information-processing is being made to do the work which was performed by the idea of the 'given' in traditional epistemology. Whether or not that is correct the suggestion made by those who have followed him in this area is that perception involves the receipt of information in a way that implies no concept use. Indeed some of those referred to in the note above adopt the extreme position that concept use is the province of belief alone and that perception does not involve concepts at all, being simply the receipt of information in the sense indicated. I shall consider such suggestions later in chapters 5 and 6.

At the moment it is perhaps desirable to consider further whether the idea of the receipt of information in the information-processing sense is in fact being made to do the work performed by the idea of the 'given' in traditional epistemology; and indeed whether the idea in question has any epistemological role at all. Evans (p.226) makes clear that he does not think that beliefs about objects come about or arise from any consideration of the informational state which is set up in perception, whereas on at least some traditional epistemological views consideration of sense-data *is* involved in this way, in that sense-data provide the basis for an inference to the nature of the physical objects with which they are associated (in whatever way the perceptual theory in question has in mind). As to what the relation actually is between the informational states produced in perception and subsequent beliefs those who espouse these notions are not exactly clear, but it is likely that they suppose that the relation is in some sense causal, since the information processing story is a modern version of those theories about the causal processes involved in perception and the coming about of perceptual beliefs which many philosophers and psychologists concerned with perception, from Aristotle onwards, have wanted to give. If that is the case, the story about information receipt and processing is epistemological only in the sense that is part of what Quine has called 'naturalized epistemology', the theory of the actual coming about of knowledge via natural psychological processes.

Informational states in no sense constitute a 'given' in the sense appropriate to classical epistemology. If there is information processing involved in the causal processes underlying perception, as may well be the case, and if the content of that information has nothing to do with any concepts which we have, which must be so given the sense of 'information' involved, that is a quite different issue from any which has been relevant to theories of sense-data. The informational states are, to use the now rather hackneyed example used in this context, like the states of a tree-trunk, its rings, in giving information about the age of the tree because there is a simple law-like connection between the two factors. It is true that those rings give information to us because of that law-like connection, and the informational states produced by the stimulation of our sense-organs could similarly provide information to a possible interpreter who knows of the law-like connection between them and some subsequent states of our system. But they do not provide information *to the perceiver whose system it is* in the same way; they are simply part of the causal processes which enable that perceiver to perceive. The informational states do not constitute data for the perceiver.

None of this belies the fact that we do or can receive information, in the ordinary sense of 'information', when we perceive things. We can perceive things *as* such and suches, and we may, if all is well, come to see *that* they are such and such. The former involves bringing the things in question under certain concepts, which of course may or may not be valid; the latter presupposes that this is in fact valid, and in the perception we come to know that this is the case. Perceiving-that is thus a form of coming to know, in which we come to know directly by the use of our senses. I say 'directly' because we might conceivably come to know something by the use of our senses when we acquire the knowledge through an inference from something that we notice about our senses or sense-experiences. We might, for example, know that a certain kind of flash in the periphery of our vision is produced by a reflection from a certain object when we are in a certain position; then when we experience the flash we might justifiably infer that the object is there, and might rightly be said to know that it is there. It is less clear that we should be justified in saying that we perceived that the object is there, although in certain circumstances that might be acceptable. At all events we need to distinguish that case from one in which perceive that the object is there without our having to infer that fact from anything. That is important because the fact that we can perceive that something is the case without this involving an inference indicates that not all perceiving-that depends on further data. Moreover, if it is thought that such cases must therefore themselves constitute data for those cases which do involve inference, it has to be pointed out that the cases in question do not comprise a class members of which have anything significant in common apart from the fact that they do not involve inference. The identification of forms of direct perception in this sense does not entail the sort of thing which Moore and others spoke of when they talked of direct perception as a way of specifying sense-data. The fact that we can come to know things without inference is no basis for belief in absolute givens.

Apart from the influence of epistemological theories which suggest (wrongly, as I have insisted) that knowledge requires a foundation in something absolutely indubitable or incorrigible, the impetus towards a belief in the 'given' stems from two connected things which imply that perception is not simply a matter of judgment on our part. The first is that we do have certain sensory experiences when we perceive, and the second is that those experiences and indeed perception in general are the result of certain causal processes. The two factors are connected in that the sensory experiences could scarcely be conceived to occur unless they were set up in us as a result of effects on our sense-organs, and because, on the other hand, it is not evident that all aspects of perception are simply the result of such causal processes. As I shall indicate further in chapter 8, we have to learn to see things as we do, and such learning, however dependent it is on causal processes, is not simply a matter of them. The sensory experiences of which I have spoken have at their core, arguably, sensations. By 'sensations' I do not mean anything like sense-data, but what, if anything, corresponds in the case of senses other than touch to the bodily sensations which touch depends on. That there are such sensations as a constituent part of perception was argued by Thomas Reid, as I noted in chapter 1. Perhaps unfortunately, Reid went on to distinguish between original and acquired perceptions, the first of which are, as he put it, suggested by sensations. These perceptions are the product of nature; the suggestion in question is natural, and Reid even speaks of there being involved a 'judgment of nature', an idea which is reminiscent of Malebranche's natural judgments. The main locus for this way of thinking in Reid is space perception; for Reid supposes, following Berkeley, that we naturally perceive spherical objects, for example, as two-dimensionally round and come to perceive their third-dimensional characteristics as the result of experience, i.e. through learning, as Berkeley claimed, by means of touch or bodily movement. Like Berkeley too, Reid says that the original perceptions suggest the acquired ones, although this kind of suggestion cannot be, as is that involved between sensations and original perceptions, a natural one. This part of Reid's thinking is thus rather confusing and arguably undermines the good work done by distinguishing sensation from perception so clearly.

I shall consider sensations and sensory experience further in the next chapter, and try to deal with the part played by causality in the following one.

Notes

1 The phrase 'directly present to consciousness' is used by H.H. Price in his (1932), *Perception*, Methuen: London, p.3 with reference to the example of the perception of a tomato directly in front of one. The phrase 'directly apprehended is used by G.E. Moore in his (1953), *Some Main Problems of Philosophy*, Allen and Unwin: London, lectures given in 1910–11, with reference to the perception of an envelope presented to his audience.

2 See e.g. Ayer, A.J. (1956), *The Problem of Knowledge*, Penguin Books: Harmondsworth, ch. 3, (iii).

3 Ayer, A.J. (1947), *Foundations of Empirical Knowledge*, Macmillan: London, p.57. J.L. Austin was scathing about this idea in his (1962), *Sense and Sensibilia*, Clarendon Press: Oxford.

4 Grice, H.P. (1961), 'The causal theory of perception', *PASS*, 35, pp.121–52, reprinted many times, including in Warnock, G.J. (ed.) (1967), *The Philosophy of Perception*, OUP: Oxford, pp.85–112, to which version all subsequent references will be made.

5 See Russell, Bertrand (1912), *The Problems of Philosophy*, OUP: Oxford, ch.5. It has to be noted that, at any rate at that time, Russell thought that there was knowledge by acquaintance of other items apart from sense-data, including universals and the self.

6 Evans, Gareth (1982), *The Varieties of Reference*, Clarendon Press: Oxford. For other discussions of the idea see Peacocke, Christopher (1983), *Sense and Content*, Clarendon Press: Oxford and other writings by him subsequently, including papers by him and Tim Crane in Crane, Tim (ed.) (1992), *The Contents of Experience: Essays on Perception*, CUP: Cambridge. See also Crane, Tim (1988), 'The Waterfall Illusion', *Analysis*, 48, pp.142ff.; Martin, M.G.F. (1992), 'Perception, Concepts and Memory', *Philosophical Review*, 101, pp.745–63; Davies, Martin (1991), 'Individualism and Perceptual Content', *Mind*, 100, pp.461–84; Millar, Alan (1991), 'Concepts, Experience and Inference', *Mind*, 100, pp.495–505. I have criticised the whole trend in my (1994), 'Perception, Sensation and Non-Conceptual Content', *The Philosophical Quarterly*, 44, pp.139–53.

Chapter 3
Sensations and appearances

One way, perhaps the best way, of getting an insight into perceptual experience is to consider its simplest and perhaps most primitive manifestations. Aristotle said that touch was the most fundamental sense, such that without it an animal dies (meaning both the biological fact, if it is one, that animal life depends for its continuance on a connection with the environment and that an animal without touch is not really an animal, but at best something like a vegetable). But touch, if this term is used to cover the bodily senses in general, is not really a single thing, and what we ordinarily mean by tactual perception, the result of, perhaps, exploration by touch and tactual contact, is not the most fundamental form of perceptual experience. Let us consider, as a way of illustrating this point, feelings of warmth and cold, feelings which are clearly and essentially bodily.

We can of course feel warm without feeling anything warm and without our bodies feeling to us or to anyone else warm. Feeling cold is quite compatible with having a fever so that our bodies have a rise in temperature and feel so to the touch. Equally, however, we often feel warm because of a rise in the ambient temperature which warms our bodies. If we put a hand into warm water the hand may come to feel warm both to us and to others who make contact with it. Or it may feel warm if touched by our other hand. But the way in which the original hand feels warm to us is not the same as the way in which it feels warm to others or to our other hand which has not been put in the water. I do not have in mind here the point invoked by the British Empiricists as grounds for undermining the objectivity of the property of warmth – that water may be felt as warm or cold, depending on the initial temperature of the hand that is put into it – although it is clear that this is a particular example of what is sometimes called perceptual relativity. Rather, I am concerned to point out that when we put a hand into warm water we may, if our hand is initially of a lower temperature, have a feeling in the hand which might genuinely be called a feeling of warmth, akin to but not quite the same as the feeling we have when we feel warm. But we are not necessarily thereby feeling the water as warm, let alone feeling our hand as warm, as we might do if we felt it with the other hand. Feeling something as warm is a perceptual phenomenon, whereas having a feeling of warmth in a part of our body is not yet that.

Is, however, the feeling of warmth the same as or like what we have in our other hand when we feel the initial hand as warm? One thing is obvious, and this is that a feeling of warmth is often likely to be more diffuse than the feeling produced through touching something warm. It might be argued, however, that in such cases it is no more diffuse than when we have a bodily feeling produced by a warm ambient medium, when the feeling produced is not particularly localised. The effects of localised stimulation of nerve-endings in the skin may in any case be somewhat paradoxical, as it is well known that any kind of pressure on certain points on the skin may produce feelings of cold, so that such feelings, if localised in this way, are not necessarily caused by anything cold. Feelings of warmth are often likely to be connected with certain conditions of both the skin and the sub-cutaneous area – expanded blood vessels and so on – so that they are more than likely to have a certain diffuseness in consequence. We tend to speak of feeling warm all over or in a certain area of the body, but not at a very precise point. None of this, however, rules out the possibility of a localised feeling of warmth, like the so-called paradoxical cold spots. So, to return to the main point at issue, is a feeling of warmth, whether localised or diffuse, like or the same as the feeling produced by a warm object or ambient medium?

One might perhaps put the question in another way, by asking whether feeling something as warm involves having a feeling of warmth? That question is arguably different from asking whether in those circumstances one has a warm feeling. I pointed out some years ago, and have repeated the point more recently,[1] that the words which we use to describe sensations normally depend on analogies with physical processes, but not necessarily and perhaps not characteristically, the processes which cause the sensations. Thus a burning sensation is so called because of an analogy with the process of burning; it may, so to speak, glow. But the actual process of burning does not necessarily produce burning sensations. A warm feeling, if one can give sense to that expression in distinction from that referring to a feeling of warmth, would depend on some analogy between the quality of that feeling and what we experience warmth (in objects) to be like. It is not clear that when we feel something as warm we necessarily have a warm feeling in that sense. But to characterise a feeling as a feeling of warmth is to characterise it in terms of a quality of its possible object. That object is only possible because in saying that we have a feeling of warmth we are not committing ourselves as to whether any actual object with that quality exists. As I said earlier, to have a feeling of warmth is not necessarily to feel anything as warm, any more than, say, to have a red after-image is necessarily to see anything as red (although we may do so if we project the after-image on to some actual surface). To characterise a feeling as one of warmth is to characterise it in perceptual terms, but not necessarily to indicate that any actual perception has taken place.

None of this quite answers the question whether the feeling of warmth that one gets when putting one's hand in warm water is like the feeling one gets in the other hand when one then feels the hand so warmed. It does not even quite answer the question whether feeling the warm hand with the other hand does produce a feeling of warmth in it at all. As far as concerns the first question, it is clear that the diffuseness of the feeling resulting from the fact that the hand is immersed in warm water, which thus surrounds it, makes a great difference to the character of the feeling. There is likely, for example, to be no sharp boundary between the area affected by the warm medium and the rest of the skin, since the warmth will be conducted away from the area directly affected by the underlying blood-vessels. By contrast, when one feels the hand so warmed with the other hand, the feelings of warmth are likely to be mixed up with other tactual sensations, so that they do not come, so to speak, pure. Nevertheless, to turn to the second question, there does not seem to be good reason for denying that the sensations involve feelings of warmth, whatever else they involve. It remains the case, however, that feeling the hand as warm is more than having those sensations. To so feel it is to perceive the hand as having a certain property, which, as it happens, is similar to one possessed by other warm objects. One might say that the hand has a certain 'appearance', in so feeling warm, except that the term 'appearance' has its most obvious place in connection with visual phenomena.

Generalising from one sense to another has certain hazards. The feelings of warmth with which I started were non-perceptual, and I have already moved from that case to one in which perception takes place, tactual perception, arguing that such perception nevertheless involves similar, if not identical, feelings. But touch is a contact sense, involving no obvious medium, though it involves the body (something that led Aristotle to maintain, on the assumption that every sense involves a medium, that the flesh was the medium of touch so that the organ of touch must be something else – as he supposed, the heart). Taste similarly involves contact with a part of the body, the tongue, but that part of the body has a kind of sensitivity that is different from other parts of the body; moreover the contact in question may depend on the presence of a liquid. Similar things can be said, *mutatis mutandis* of smell and the part played in this by the nose. But the object that emits the smells in question does not have to have direct contact with the nose, even if particles of some substance coming from it have to have such contact. The sense of smell is not, strictly speaking, a contact sense, such that it depends on immediate contact between an object and the sense-organ. There is no good reason, however, to deny that the perceptions involved in the case of both taste and smell, and the consequent gustatory and olfactory appearances of the objects of taste and smell, depend on the production by those objects of certain characteristic sensations, which are not the same as, though involved in, those appearances. Moreover, the identification of those sensations does not present real problems.

The situation is not so obvious in the case of hearing. The mechanics of hearing are clearly more complicated than is the case with the senses so far surveyed.

Vibrations at certain frequencies occurring in objects set up vibrations in a medium, such as air, and these have their effect on a certain section of the cochlea of the ear. But all this is complicated by the fact that we have two ears, enabling hearing of both the direction and distance of the source of the sound and of the spatial distribution of sounds. Moreover, sounds are perceived to have timbres as well as pitches, volumes and other auditory properties of sounds. On top of all that what is heard can be heard as having a certain significance, as is the case with the hearing of music and paradigmatically in the hearing of speech. This very complexity of the phenomena and function of hearing entails that there is normally no place for attention to anything that might be thought of as auditory sensations. There can be the kind of savouring of a sound which is parallel to the savouring of a taste or smell, but that involves an abstraction from the complexity of what is there to be heard and a concentration on one element in what might be called the auditory field in isolation from other elements. This is still not a concentration on a sensation or sensations in abstraction from anything perceptual. Sometimes, of course, at an extreme of intensity, at, say, excessive loudness, the purely sensory aspect may become evident in the approximation of the experience to pain. At other times, nothing of the kind is normally evident. But that is not a reason for denying the existence of sensations in connection with hearing; it is rather that the the the orientation towards sounds and their origins that we have in the use of hearing makes any consideration of sensations out of place, unnatural, and, as a result, difficult if not impossible.

When one turns to vision those complications are magnified still further. Apart from the various dimensions of colour, brightness and contrast that the visual world possesses, its spatiality is extremely complex, and there is a natural, if learned, connection between what we see of that spatiality and our ability to move through a world of spatially distributed objects. Indeed our very ability to move our eyes, while the rest of our body is stationary, introduces a factor which is not present in the other senses, except in what is possible in touch through the movement of our limbs and in hearing, and to some extent smell, through the limited ability to turn our head. Thus in vision there is a literal point of view, which has more limited analogues in the case of the other senses which I have just mentioned. Indeed, to some thinkers it has appeared that the world is simply a visual world, and the epistemology of perception has tended to be a theory of what knowledge is available through vision. But this, while understandable, is a mistake, as is the suggestion[2] that there are no visual sensations. It is true that such sensations must have a very complex organisation, and the individuation of any distinct sensation will be impossible; but that realisation does not rob vision of a sensory aspect. Visual sensations, if one can allow the term, are not visual sense-data, and form no epistemological basis for perception of the world. But they, as with the other senses, give vision the experiential character that it has.

Christopher Peacocke, at an early stage of his writings on perception,[3] went part of the way to this conclusion, arguing that here are reasons for supposing that there is a sensory element in perception. Unfortunately, there are two respects in which what he says is wrong. First, he claims that the sensory element in perception can be picked out via what he calls 'primed predicates'; thus the sensory element involved in the perception of a red thing can be picked out by a primed version of 'red' – 'red'. The thought is that there is some connection of meaning between 'red' and its primed version, the only question being how that connection runs and which term has priority in meaning. As I have already pointed out, however, the way in which terms describing sensations normally have meaning is not via any analogy or other similar connection between the characteristics of the sensation and those of what produces it (as between the characteristics of the sensation involved in perceiving something red and that redness), but via an analogy between the characteristics of the sensation and some other identifiable process (as between the characteristics of a burning sensation and the phenomenon of burning). Burning does not necessarily produced burning sensations; no more does a red colour necessarily produce visual sensations which can be described by a terms which has any connection with 'red'.

Second, Peacocke seems to suggest that in order to perceive something as F we need to be sensitive to F experiences in some way (and, however this works out, it has to do with the connection that he takes to exist between the applications of primed and unprimed predicates). But, in any sense of 'sensitive' that seems intelligible, being sensitive to the characteristics of the sensations which we are having in perceiving something as F would be inimical to our perceiving something as F. To go back to the case of touch, where the situation is at its clearest, if we are sensitive to the sensations which we are having in our finger-tips when passing them over a surface with a certain texture, we are likely to be *in*sensitive to the actual perceived properties of that texture. Thomas Reid said, in a similar context, that sensations *suggest* to us the corresponding perception, because sensations are a *natural sign* of perceived qualities of an object. Whatever Reid meant by 'suggest' (a term taken over from Berkeley's discussion of distance perception) and 'natural sign', there can be no implication in their use that one has to learn the connection between characteristics of sensations and characteristics of what causes them; nor is the relation between sensations and perception in any way inferential. In that Reid was right.

But Reid also defined a sensation as an act of mind that has no object other than itself. He was right in thus maintaining that sensations do not have objects as perception does (they are not, to use the jargon of a later age, intentional). But there is also an implication in what he said that they do have objects nevertheless, i.e. themselves. The most obvious way of taking this is as a claim that in having a sensation one is necessarily conscious of having it. That claim is valid in the case of the most obvious of our feelings, but there are occasions even in the case of, say, pain when we might be inclined to say that when our attention was elsewhere we still had the pain without being aware of doing so. The fact that some pains may be so acute as to make it impossible for our attention to be elsewhere does not go against that point. Hence there need be no objection to the claim that in normal perception we are having sensations without being directly aware of them because our attention is directed to the objects of the perception. In that case it is false that in perceiving something as red we are sensitive to any sensations what we are having in the process, whether or not the characteristics of those sensations are to be characterised as red. That is not the way in which the sensations contribute to the total perceptual experience.

In what way, then, do they so contribute? In order to see something as red that something has to look or appear red to us (something, incidentally, that is not true of our seeing *that* something is red, since seeing that something is red may well involve an inference from something else about the object). Something can look red to us without our having any belief or inclination to believe that it is red, even if our beliefs about the properties of objects is sometimes, if not always, based upon how they look to us. To say that something looks red to us is in some way to indicate the perceptual experience that the object in question is producing in us. It is not just to say that we are having such and such sensations, since, as I have already suggested and will go on to discuss further in chapter 6, we need the concept of F for something to look or appear F to us. Nevertheless, the sensations that we are having give the perceptual experience the phenomenal character that it has. That character is part of what distinguishes, for example, looks from smells or feels, although it is not all that there is to it; there is also, amongst other things, the relation to the part of the body in which the relevant sense-organ is to be found and the perspective which this generates. For the last reason alone nobody could confuse a look with a feel or smell, and it might be thought quite unnecessary even to contemplate the possibility. On the other hand, Aristotle, for one, raised the question in *De Anima* III.2 of what enables us to judge that sweet is different from white, arguing that that possibility entails a general form of sensibility (identified by many commentators, though in my opinion wrongly, with what Aristotle called the 'common sense').4

A look is a complex thing, as are the corresponding appearances in the case of the other senses. A thing's looking such and such is the correlate of our seeing it *as* such and such. I shall return to a consideration of seeing-as in chapters 6 and 7, and consider there in more detail the parts played by conceptual understanding and imagination in it. The fact that the look of a thing may be common to many people or people in general in given circumstances and the fact that what look a thing has may be an objective matter does not belie the fact that there would be no such things as looks did not we have visual experiences. Those experiences are the product of complex causal and other processes but they would not be experiences at all if they did not have a sensory component. Moreover, they would not be the kind of experiences that they are if the sensory component in question, the kinds of sensations that are involved, did not have the character that they have. It is that character which in turn gives the look its own phenomenal character, just as the bodily sensations involved in touch give a feeling of touch its own character. We do not need to be attending to the sensations for this to be the case, but the sensations have to be there.

22

Notes

1 See my (1957), 'The visual field and perception', *PASS*, 31, pp.107–24, and my (1990), *In and Out of the Black Box*, Basil Blackwell: Oxford, p.87.

2 Such as that made by Gilbert Ryle in his (1949), *The Concept of Mind*, Hutchinson: London, pp.240ff., and elsewhere.

3 Peacocke, Christopher (1983), *Sense and Content*, Clarendon Press: Oxford, chapters 1 and 2. In subsequent writings he has tended to fall more in line with cognitive science approaches to the subject, emphasising the non-conceptual content of perception.

4 See the notes on the passage in my (1968), *Aristotle's De Anima Books II and III*, Clarendon Press: Oxford, esp. p.128. I shall discuss the issue further in chapter 11.

It may seem one of the most obvious things about perception that it is subject to and in many ways the result of causal processes. For perception to occur a sense-organ must be affected by some sort of stimulation arising from energy produced by an object. Indeed, when an experience takes place which is found not to be dependent on such causal processes that is enough for the experience in question to be deemed non-perceptual, however else it is to be characterised, e.g. as an hallucination. So much is obvious, though the obviousness does not lessen the importance of the point. As noted briefly earlier, when Aristotle came to deal with perception in his *De Anima* the first thing that he noted as generally accepted was that perception consisted in 'being moved and affected' (416b33), although later (431a5) he came to qualify that assertion, because of refinements that he wished to put on the account required to characterise adequately the processes involved; also perhaps he came to attach increasing importance to the role of judgment in perception. As far as concerns the processes involved he wanted to emphasise the point that in perception something, the object (which is always required) actualises a potentiality which is already there in the sense-organ. But whether or not that is an adequate account of what is involved, it is clear in any case that such an actualisation of a potentiality involves a causal process. Hence, the role of causality is unmistakable.

It is also true, however, that saying that an object actualises a potentiality in a sense-organ may be thought obscurantist unless it is made clear just what that potentiality is and how the actualisation of it takes place. On neither of these points is Aristotle entirely clear. He tends to say such things as that in perception the sense-organ1 receives the form of the object without its matter, although he adds that for this to be possible the processes in question must involve a medium (as is the function of light in the case of sight) and there must also be a proportionate relation or mean (a *logos*) between the state of the object and that of the sense-organ (so that, in effect, the stimulation is neither too great nor too little). Towards the end of the section (II.12) where the formula is introduced, Aristotle faces the question what is the difference between e.g. smelling considered as something which we do and merely being affected by smells (as objects such as the air in the kitchen can be affected by smells). What is smelling, he asks rhetorically, apart from being affected. 'Or is smelling also perceiving, whereas the air when affected quickly becomes an object of perception? (424b16–18). Some commentators have wanted to say that Aristotle must be saying that perception also involves consciousness and that the word in the quoted sentence translated as 'perceiving' actually means consciousness. There are no good grounds for this view. Aristotle is merely reinforcing the view that while being affected in some way is necessary for perception, it is not sufficient. There are, of course, the additional factors mentioned above, but the question remains whether they are enough. It is far from obvious that they are.

The point which I mentioned earlier, the increasing emphasis that Aristotle comes to put on the role of judgment in perception, is another complicating factor, although it cannot without further argument be assumed that even if perception does involve judgment this is incompatible with the view that perception is the result of causal processes. The judgment in question might itself be brought about by whatever acts upon us when we perceive; an object might cause us to judge that it is such and such. Whether this could always be the case or merely something that happens sometimes is a question that I shall leave for now; what I shall have to say about perception and belief in chapter 5 may cast light on it. But in the history of the philosophy of perception after Aristotle theories of perception tend either to assimilate perception to sensation, thus emphasising the causal aspects which are most obvious in connection with sensation, or to assimilate it to judgment, thus making less obvious how the causal processes which seem to underlie perception are in fact connected with it.[2]

However this may be, by the time that one comes to the 17th and 18th centuries AD, when something to be called the causal theory of perception comes to be a dominant view, the situation is changed because with Descartes theories of perception also become representationalist. That is to say that, as noted in chapter 2, it became widely believed that we have access merely to the contents of our own minds, ideas or what have you, which are at best merely representations of what is in the so called external world (external not merely to our bodies, as Aristotle viewed the objects of perception, but external to our minds). With this general conception, while it was often thought that objects cause us to have such representations (even if the supposed fact that we have access only to those representations makes it difficult for us to see how we could know about this causal background), interest in the details of the causal processes involved in perception, such as those which we have noted in Aristotle's theory, tended to lessen. As noted in chapter 1, Descartes, in his *Dioptric, I,* likened vision to the use of a stick by a blind man. In the latter case details of objects are transmitted via movements in the stick, which in turn set up movements in the sense-organs and the brain; but no images are dispatched to the brain for the mind there to contemplate (cf. *Dioptric,*

IV). So it is, he thought. with perception in general. In his view, representations may be set up in the soul or mind by such movements, but the representations are not *transmitted* through whatever medium exists for different forms of perception. But if perception simply consists in the having of those representations in the soul, the causal processes are not essential to what perception is; they are merely a contingent aspect of perception. All that we need to know in order to understand what perception is is that the representations which we have are caused by things in the world. And even that is a purely contingent matter, so that, as with Berkeleian phenomenalism, it could make sense, given the presuppositions of the whole way of thinking, to deny any causal link between representations and things which are responsible for them. In that case the distinction which we take to exist between perception and the imagination will have to be made in other ways – in terms of some characteristic, such as liveliness, of perceptual representations which is, supposedly not possessed by those of the imagination.

In so far, however, as 17th and 18th century philosophers were concerned with the causal processes underlying perception, it was the Cartesian approach, already mentioned, which provided the framework for their account. As I have already made clear, all that Descartes was anxious to point out was that there was in perception some transmission of motions, according, in the case of vision, to the principles manifested in optics, including geometrical optics. There was some concern, especially in the writings of Malebranche and Berkeley,[3] as to why in some cases how we see things does not correspond to what we should expect, given optical principles. Why for example does the moon look bigger at the horizon than it does at the zenith? What explains that and other illusions? In the particular case of the zenith-horizon illusion, Berkeley appeals to the role of vapours rising from the earth affecting the appearance of the moon at the horizon; it then looks fainter, is taken to be further away and is therefore seen as bigger. (Epicurus had argued on analogous grounds that the sun must be about the same size as it appears to be, for nothing so bright could be far away!) The suggestion that the moon at the horizon is taken to be further away might seem to imply that judgment enters into the workings of perception and affects how things look. But for Berkeley it is really only a matter of one sensation affecting another. Malebranche, who also thinks that the illusion is due to the moon's being seen as further away at the horizon, puts that down to the effect of the perception of intervening objects (which are of course not there when the moon is at the zenith). But, as noted in chapter 2, he is sensitive to the point that if all this involves judgments on our part, these judgments are not what he calls 'free judgments'. They are what he calls natural judgments, and these he still regards as a form of sensation, although a complex one, and such sensations simply modify the ones received according to the principles of optics. Indeed, he says that optics in general is simply the science which covers the way in which our eyes are deceived. But this is in part because he thinks that sense-perception does not and is not designed to enable us to apprehend the truth about things; the role of the senses is is simply the preservation of the body, the maintenance of life.

The last view is clearly a very special one, though typical of the rationalists to the extent that they believed that it was reason, not sense-perception which is the source of real knowledge. But they shared with Berkeley the view that the psychology of perception, to the extent that it was concerned with the causes of perception, has to do with how one sensation affects another. This perhaps has its clearest exemplification in Berkeley's *New Theory of Vision*, the main concern of which is how we can see things as at a distance at all, given the fact that the retina of the eye is a two-dimensional surface. For, Berkeley says (*N.T.V.*, 2), 'Distance being a line directed end-wise to the eye, it projects only one point in the fund of the eye. Which point remains invariably the same, whether the distance be longer or shorter.' Berkeley's answer, in brief, is that he perception of distance is fundamentally the role of touch (this of course allowing for movement through a third dimension). The ideas of touch 'suggest' as a result of experience ideas of visual distance; one sensation, again, affects another, so that the natural sensations provided by vision are complicated by their association with those of touch.

It remains true that the causal roles noted in all this turn on what are taken to be causal connections between experiences, whether or not such connections would be shown to hold good on a well-founded psychology of perception.4 There is no attempt in these theories to try to explain, as Aristotle did, what physical and physiological conditions hold good when perception of objects takes place. On the Cartesian view, it was deemed enough to say that the movements of bodies produce movements in the sense-organs and in the brain (via movements in 'animal spirits'), and then there is the final great causal leap, whereby experiences in the form of ideas are produced in the soul.5 The ideas produced, though not transmitted, are at best representations of objects, but the only grounds for the belief that they can be that at all are to be found in the general rationalist theory, not in perception.

The representationalist theory of perception, and of the mind in general, particularly in connection with forms of idealism which the theory did much to spawn, tended to have the result that philosophers thought that the details of the causal conditions of perception had no philosophical importance or even relevance. This was true even of the sense-data philosophers who were typical of early 20th century of empiricism. However, when the idea of sense-data was thought by many to have died a natural death, there were some attempts to revive it, and one of those apparent attempts involved a concern with the causal conditions of perception which had some similarity to the concerns of Aristotle in that respect. One can construe Aristotle as attempting to spell out the necessary conditions of perception in a way that reveals them as jointly sufficient; it is this which explains his specification of things like the necessity for a medium and a proportionate relation between the states of the object and the sense-organ. What is added to this general strategy by the modern attempts to rebuild a causal theory of perception founded on something like a conception of sense-data, particularly that provided, as noted in chapter 2, by H.P. Grice,6 is derived from the belief that the necessary and sufficient conditions for the truth of a statement, including of course statements about the perception of something, give the meaning of that statement. Hence these modern versions of the causal theory of perception differ from earlier ones in explicitly connecting a theory of perception with considerations in the philosophy of language (being thus part of what has been called the 'linguistic turn').

I shall not enter here into the general question whether the meaning of a statement is always a matter of its necessary and sufficient truth-conditions. (Though where p entails q and q entails p the truth of q is a necessary and sufficient condition for the truth of p, but it is not clear that the meaning of p is the same as that of q; cf.'X is a triangle' and 'X has three sides'.) What is important for present purposes is that the Gricean causal theory of perception is meant to provide conceptually necessary and sufficient conditions for the truth of 'X perceives M' (where X is a person and M a physical object of perception), not merely contingent conditions, not even the best conditions scientifically available. Another thing which I shall not discuss further here is the claim made by Grice, and noted in chapter 2, that it is possible to set out a neutral sense of 'sense-datum', correlative with neutral senses of 'appears' or 'looks', such that the causal theory can be expressed in terms of causal relations between objects seen and sense-data for which they are responsible. All that is important here is the claim that the necessary and sufficient truth conditions for the statement 'X perceives M' are given by some story about the causal relations between M and how things appear to X.

About this certain points need to be noted:

1 It is not generally in dispute that a causal relation between the object of perception and how things appear is a necessary condition of our perceiving it.[7]
2 Given the causal relations between the object and how it appears to X, it is not necessary that the appearances should match the object. If one sees something wrongly one may still be seeing it.
3 It may often (generally?) be the case that the forms of causation which are necessary will be special. Grice thinks that it is legitimate to state the matter in a way that leaves a gap to be filled in by specialists. This is arguably unproblematic in connection with necessary conditions; it is another matter for a complete account of both necessary and sufficient conditions. For this reason Strawson argues that it is necessary to distinguish between naive and sophisticated concepts of perception, and that in the case of the former we need to mention only obvious limiting conditions, such that we cannot be said to see something which is too far away or behind masking obstacles. A reduplication of concepts of perception raises problems in itself, however, in that it provokes the questions why they are both concepts of *perception* and how far the processes of sophistication can go while retaining a connection of meaning with the naive conception. Strawson's suggestion has not met with much in the way of acceptance, considered as part of an attempt to spell out the necessary and sufficient conditions for statements about perception, although something like it is implicit in the reactions of some cognitive scientists to other aspects of so-called folk psychology, to the extent that they distinguish technical concepts of psychology from those employed in everyday life.

Given all this, one can now ask whether M's causing something to appear to X can be sufficient for it to be true that X perceives M. On the face of it, that claim is very implausible and Grice admitted as much (p.104). For sufficiency one needs to restrict the kind of causation in question. Grice therefore says as follows (p.105):

> I suggest that the best procedure for the Causal Theorist is to indicate the mode of causal connexion by examples; to say that, for an object to be perceived by X, it is sufficient that it should be causally involved in the generation of some sense-impression by X in the kind of way in which, for example, when I look at my hand in good light, my hand is causally responsible for its looking to me as if there were a hand before me, or in which ... (and so on), *whatever that kind of way may be*; and to be enlightened on that question one must have recourse to a specialist.

There have been and can be objections to this account of the causal relation in respect of (a) the example itself and (b) what it allows in the way of extension to other examples. Let us consider these two forms of objection in turn.

(a) The example by itself is not good enough to specify a *kind* of sufficient causal relation at all. All that we are told is that my hand is responsible for it looking to me as if there is a hand before me when my hand is in good light. But, clearly, when my hand is before me and in good light it need not cause it to look like that at all. Moreover, the specification of the example is compatible with its *not* being the case that I perceive M, so that its looking that way because of M is not sufficient for that purpose. One needs for both reasons to be told exactly what kind of causal relation is involved.

(b) How could one generalise from the example in way that is non-circular? How, that is, could one specify the ways in which the causality takes place without saying that it is one of the ways that is in place when X perceives M (cf. Strawson, p.73)? Most of subsequent discussion of Grice's argument has been directed to this point, but how, in any case, is one to generalise from an inadequately specified example? Must not one have some definite principle for selecting the appropriate causal relations? Strawson's distinction between naive and sophisticated concepts of perception and his attempt to provide what he calls 'tautologies' by way of conditions for the former is not in the spirit of Grice's programme, and is in any case subject to the objections, already noted, about the reduplication of concepts of perception. Pears (p.33) tries to specify the appropriate causal line by saying that it is any that reliably performs the function of delivering matching experiences; but there might be such causal lines, e.g. when matching experiences are supplied by a god-like being, without this amounting to perception.

An important reason why, while it seems quite right to say that unless certain causal conditions are satisfied one is not perceiving (a point about necessary conditions), it does not seem possible to state in a satisfactory way a set of conditions which are sufficient, is that the concept of perception is not entirely causal. In effect, this point was becoming evident to Aristotle, when he came to emphasis the part played by judgment in perception. Even when 'judgment' is not quite the right word to use, there may be forms of concept use exercised by the perceiver, and even if causal conditions involving the object may provide the occasion for these, it may not be right to say that they are caused by it. For one thing, it is likely that such forms of concept use will have to be learnt, as suggested in chapter 2. Moreover, it is not just the case that one has to learn to see things in certain ways; in the case of some things we may have to learn to see them at all. For example, there may be something hidden in a complex environment, like a figure in a puzzle-picture; in order to see it there may well be certain things that we have to learn to do, e.g. pay particular attention to certain aspects of the scene, set aside misleading indications, and so on. It might be argued that not all perception is like that, and of course it isn't. Nevertheless, the use of concepts to characterise and identify what is there does generally presuppose learning and, moreover, a form of agency on our part. Such factors seem quite uncausal, however they are to be fitted into a general account of what happens. The place of causality in perception is unmistakable, but it is not all that there is.

Before passing on, however, it would be as well to note one other thing. In discussing the role of causality in perception I have concentrated on its general function. But it is clear enough that particular causal circumstances often affect *how* we see things, and causal considerations may have to be invoked to explain many (though not all) illusions. Causal factors also put limits on what it is possible for us to perceive in various circumstances. Such things have to be noted, even if detailing them is not necessary to a *general* theory of perception. One point of this kind should perhaps, however, be mentioned here. Perception normally involves a point of view (or what corresponds to that in the case of senses other than vision). [8] Our ability to turn our head or eyes in a given direction, so as to take in one aspect of what is perceivable rather than another, depends on complex causal processes. The stereo effect manifested in hearing and the general ability to hear sounds as coming from a particular direction depends, not merely on an ability to turn the head, but on the disparities involved in the stimulation of one ear at a different time from that of the other. Consider too the causal role of retinal disparity in enabling visual perception of the distance of things. While causality is not everything in perception, it would be a gross mistake to ignore it. Other points about causality will emerge in the following.

Notes

1   Where he first introduces this formula (424a17) he says that it is the *sense* which so receives the form of the object, but, although this has been a matter for some argument, it is clear that he means the sense-organ, and in other passages (424b23 and 435a22) he says as much. The trouble is that commentators have not always been willing to regard the processes involved as

simply physiological. See my (1968), *Aristotle's De Anima Books II and III*, Clarendon Press: Oxford, p.113.

2 For a history of these trends see my (1961), *Sensation and Perception*, Routledge and Kegan Paul: London.

3 Malebranche, Nicholas, *De la Recherche de la Vérité*, I.6ff. and Berkeley, George, *The New Theory of Vision*.

4 J.S. Gibson argued in his first book (1950), *The Perception of the Visual World*, Houghton Mifflin: Boston, for example, that things at varying distances from us project on to the retina of the eye in such a way as to form varying gradients, so that information about distance is available, even though the retina of the eye comprises a two-dimensional surface. But that of course does not explain how we see the distance of things at all, only, given that we do, something that contributes to that possibility.

5 Malebranche, an occasionalist, thought that the idea of a causal connection between bodies and ideas in the soul was unintelligible, and held that God produces the ideas in the soul on the occasion of the bodily occurrences which are, as we think, relevant.

6 Grice, H.P. (1961), 'The causal theory of perception', *PASS*, 35, pp.121–52 (reprinted in Warnock, G.J. (ed.) (1967), *The Philosophy of Perception*, OUP: Oxford, pp.85–112. References will be to this version.). Grice's paper was replied to by Alan R. White in the same places. See also Strawson, P.F. (1974), 'Causation in perception' in his *Freedom and Resentment*, Methuen: London, pp.66–84; Pears, D.F. (1976), 'The causal conditions of perception', *Synthese*, 33, pp.25ff.; and Snowdon, Paul (1980/1), 'Perception, vision and causation', *PASS*, 81, pp.175–92.

7 This has sometimes been denied. See e.g. Dretske, Fred I. (1969), *Seeing and Knowing*, Routledge and Kegan Paul: London, pp.50ff. Dretske thinks that if someone was able to report accurately what is the other side of an opaque wall, we should eventually be forced to say that he was perceiving it.

8 For points of view see also pp.33 and 133.

It is sometimes said that seeing is believing. It is clear, however, that that is not always true, even if it is a major function of perception to provide us with information, and thereby beliefs and knowledge, about the world. In the case of sensory illusions, like the well-known Müller-Lyer illusion, in which when arrow-heads pointing in opposing directions are attached to the ends of lines of equal length they look of different length, we may well not believe or indeed have any inclination to believe what we see. Moreover, if it is claimed that at any rate we would believe that the lines are of different length did we not know to the contrary, it can be replied that the only possible explanation of that fact is that we should so believe because that is how the lines look, i.e. that is how we see them. It is not even true, as Reid seemed to suggest in his account of the factors involved in perception that when we see something we have a belief in the existence of that thing, even if, as again Reid insisted, the belief is not the result of an inference. We can be said quite properly to see things in, for example, the fire or in the clouds (i.e. in a diffuse and unclear background) which we would quite willingly admit are not really there. Someone can see a person in a crowd without having any belief in the existence of that person there.

These considerations are enough in themselves to rule out any attempt to analyse perception directly in terms of belief, although it needs to be emphasised again that that does not go against the point that perception has the production of beliefs as one of its main functions.[1] The connection between perception and belief is more complex than one which makes the first directly explicable in terms of the second. However, it may still be arguable that, if in the Müller-Lyer illusion, for example, I need not believe that the lines are of different length in order to see them as such, I must nevertheless believe something. For one thing, if I see X as F I must have at least some belief about what it is for something to be F (for at least this is involved in having a concept of F and it is difficult to see how one could see something as F unless one had at least this much of a concept of F). Hence, it begins to look as if the question whether a form of perception is, as it has been put, epistemic (i.e. involves knowledge or belief) is a relative matter, depending on the distance of the belief in question from the actual perception.[2]

However, claims have been made for the existence of non-epistemic seeing, completely belief-independent seeing (or indeed perception in general) in an absolute sense. The best example of such a claim is that made by Fred Dretske in chapter 2 of his first book *Seeing and Knowing*.[3]

His main purpose in that book is to give an account of 'seeing that'; that is to say, an account of what it is for someone to see that something is the case. (It is one of the great virtues of the book that it shows how wide the range of instances can be in which it is appropriate to say of someone that he or she saw that p; it includes all those cases in which the claimed seeing depends on instruments of one kind or another, so that one could see, for example, things detectable only by scientific means.) Since, if I see that p, it follows that I know that p, even if I have acquired that knowledge by one special way – by visual perception – an account of 'seeing that' is *ipso facto* an account of a form of knowledge. Thus Dretske's theses are part of the general enterprise of providing an analysis of knowledge, of providing an account in terms of truth-conditions of what it is to know that p. This has become an elaborate growth-industry within philosophy in recent years, and Dretske has gone on to make other contributions to it. That is not my present concern. What is to the point here is that if 'seeing that' is a form of knowledge it is necessary, if an adequate account of it is to be given, to explain what makes it the particular *form* of knowledge that it is; that is, to explain what makes it a perceptual form. Dretske thinks that to this end it is necessary to set out as one of the truth-conditions for 'S sees that p' some reference to a form of perception which is non-epistemic. This is a form of perception such that S can be said to see an object, D, without his or her thereby seeing that anything is the case at all. This would be an instance of non-epistemic seeing in an absolute sense.

One might perhaps wonder why Dretske does not do the sort of thing that I have been doing in this book – set out the sorts of things which hold good of a perceiver, such as the having of experiences, the satisfaction of causal conditions, and so on, which perception presupposes. But Dretske is less concerned to say what is presupposed by perception in general than to make clear what are the necessary and sufficient truth-conditions for any particular perceptual claim of the form 'S sees that p'. To this end it is enough that an account of what it is to know that p is supplemented by whatever makes it clear that the form of knowledge is perceptual, as opposed to being derived from some other source. If there were non-epistemic seeing in an absolute sense, such that it is thereby quite independent of any knowledge or belief relevant to 'p', that might be enough to do the trick. What Dretske wants, therefore, is a something about the seeing of the object, D, which 'p' is about, which explains why the seeing that p is a case of *seeing*, and such that the account of seeing D excludes reference to anything to do with 'p'.

Dretske finds the non-epistemic seeing that he wants in what he takes to be instances of visual differentiation in which something is simply differentiated visually from its immediate environment, and nothing more. His formal account of that is given on pp.20ff of his book, and he specifies five 'salient features' of it. They are:

1 the visual differentiation of D entails that D looks some way to S;
2 D's looking some way to S does *not* mean that 'it looks to S *as though* (as if) D (or something) were C'. (That is to say that is is a function of the experiences of S, not his or her beliefs.);
3 D need not be a physical object;
4 'differentiated' is meant to describe a particular way of D's looking to S, i.e. as distinguished from its environment;
5 the visual differentiation may or may not involve prosthetic devices, such as glasses.

It might be agreed that something can be visually differentiated from its environment in such a way that it looks such, i.e. differentiated, to the perceiver, *and nothing more*. In that case, however, the perceiver would still require the concept of difference in order so to perceive it. To put the matter in another way – Dretske insists that in the case of non-epistemic seeing the object, D, whatever it is, must look some way to S; but that is impossible unless S has the concept of the way in question. To have the concept of X entails at least knowing what it is for something to be X. If that is right, the perceiver must have some knowledge in order even to have the form of non-epistemic perception that Dretske has in mind. One is not, by emphasis on non-epistemic seeing (seeing n, as opposed to seeing e, as Dretske formulates it) pointing to a form of perception which presupposes no knowledge of the world. It might be objected to this that Dretske does not suppose otherwise, since the aim of his analysis is to isolate a truth-condition for 'S sees that p', which makes clear that it is seeing that is in question without begging the question by presupposing the knowledge that is involved in seeing that p itself. Other forms or items of knowledge would not matter for these purposes. However, in that case the non-epistemic seeing would not have to be non-epistemic in any absolute sense. Why should one not say simply that in order for S to see that p (where 'p' has something to do with an object D) D must look some way to S (and one could then go on to try to make clear what is involved in things looking such and such to a perceiver)?

In fact Dretske has another reason for arguing as he does, a reason which is brought out by the concluding words of his discussion in chapter 2 of his book (p.77). He wishes also to combat the view that we are inevitably subject to perceptual relativity, as he thinks might be suggested by the view that '*what we see*, in an *epistemic* way, can be influenced by all those variables that are capable of influencing what we believe (p.76) (and that includes, as he goes on to make clear, one's past experience and conceptual categories). Such perceptual relativity might be thought to undermine belief in the objectivity and publicity of what we perceive. But, he says, 'The objectivity and publicity of this world resides in the fact that we can all, *regardless* of our conceptual background, associative talents, inferential skill, or past experience, *see n* the same objects and events'. It is not at all clear, however, that much, if anything, on that score is achieved by the thought that we can all differentiate visually the same objects. Since we vary in the acuity of our sense-organs and the ability to use them, it seems doubtful that we can all, in fact, differentiate the same objects. But even if we could, that would do little to show the objectivity of what we see, whatever it shows about its publicity. For all that one could be sure about would be that common and objective ways of seeing can possibly exist, not that they do in fact exist. Nevertheless, it is clear that for the argument to start at all it is necessary to suppose the existence of a form of commerce with the world which is absolutely independent of all beliefs and knowledge; hence non-epistemic perception in an absolute sense. But if perception does depend on a form of commerce with the world (and that might be thought obvious), why is that not achieved by sensation and the causal processes which produce it. We do not need a special form of perception for that purpose, a special form of perception on which all other forms are based.

There has been some debate in the literature 4 about whether there can be epistemic perception without the existence of non-epistemic perception, and vice versa. What I have said is not a contribution to that debate, which is arguably misconstrued. What I have been concerned with is whether perception presupposes epistemic factors in some way, not necessarily factors which are *perceptually* epistemic, and I have suggested that Dretske gives us no reason to suppose otherwise. If perception is concept-dependent, then perception cannot take place except in knowers and believers, since the very possession of concepts implies forms of knowledge and belief. This has an importance for other questions, including the relation of perception to the growth of understanding, but it does not undermine the concept of perception itself or make it difficult to understand its objectivity.

Two things are, however, clear. (a) Unless perception had some connection with belief it would not be perception. A suggested concept of perception which implied otherwise would not really be a concept of perception. but, at best one of sensation only. Perception is connected with belief, first, because it presupposes it via concepts, and, second, because within the general economy which makes up the mind an important function of perception is to enable us to form beliefs about the world. (b) Given a general concept of perception of this kind, it is quite possible for there to be forms of perception which are not a direct function of any beliefs, however much belief is presupposed in more indirect ways. That is to say that the reason why we see things in such and such ways may be found in some cases not in beliefs which we have, but in other conditions of perception, e.g. in features of the causal circumstances. That is what makes it possible to distinguish a whole class of sensory illusions, as opposed to illusions which are due to distorted beliefs. In the case of sensory illusions (of which the Müller-Lyer illusion may be an instance) we should have to look, for an explanation of them, to some factor or factors in the causal processes which lead to them, not to any beliefs which the perceivers have. Equally, perception can occur without this involving the conveying of information about the world, to the extent that perception has a purely aesthetic aspect. But none of this goes against the suggestion that there can be no perception unless the perceiver is a knower.

It might be objected, however, that none of this quite explains the relation between perception and belief when that relation exists. As I indicated in chapter 2, there are some, particularly those influenced by conceptions of information-processing, who wish to keep perception and belief separate, maintaining that the content of perception is non-conceptual and that conceptual content is restricted to belief. Earlier, as I indicated in chapter 1, the psychologist, J.J. Gibson, maintained that perception had nothing to do with belief or concepts, and that the idea of the receipt of information in perception is enough.5 However, the notion of information employed by him is, on his own admission, more or less the ordinary one and certainly not that involve in technical information-theory. But in the ordinary sense of 'information' to get information about something is either to derive a belief from it or to regard it as a possible object of belief. Those who put all the weight on the idea of information-processing in the technical sense cannot be dealt with in that way, and if they regard perception and belief as quite distinct this must be regarded as putting a limitation on perception.6 To speak of seeing as believing at all would on that view be either to use a mere metaphor or to be a grossly shorthand way of putting the point that the processes which perception involves may sometimes result in belief. On the latter interpretation the processes involved in perception will be purely causal, their role being merely to produce in the brain what are in some sense representations of the objects which are their causes.

Most of the argument in this connection has been about the sort of content that perception has, it being claimed that perceptual content is non-conceptual. I shall return to that point in the next chapter. Here the relevant issue is that this point about content leads to a sharp separation between perception and belief, in that the content of the latter is, by agreement, conceptual. Unless, however, concepts themselves can be construed as having the same kind of status as the supposed perceptual representations this will make the relationship between perception and belief mysterious or at best one of unexplained and perhaps inexplicable causality. For the relationship will be one between two quite different things. If, on the other hand, the content of perception is itself at least partly conceptual a relationship with belief is already presupposed in perception itself; for, as I believe, something can have conceptual content only if it somehow presupposes knowledge and thereby belief. Further consideration of the place of concepts in perception must be reserved for the next chapter. It is enough here to note that even if there is a problem about bringing together in an intelligible way the experiential, purely sensory, aspect of perception with its belief aspect, there is not a problem about the relationship between perception itself and belief. Even if perception can sometimes be non-epistemic, it is often epistemic, and even non-epistemic perception is impossible except in a knower and believer.

I said that there might be thought to be a problem about bringing together in an intelligible way the sensory and belief aspects of perception. It is clear enough that they cannot be thought of as being brought together in a purely additive way. If one puts alongside, so to speak, a sensation and a belief – one, say, about the cause of the sensation – one does not thereby arrive at a perception. If one has a pain in a certain part of one's body and believes that it is caused by a pin sticking into one, that is not enough for it to be true of one that one is perceiving, i.e. feeling, the pin. It is also necessary that in having the pain one's attention should be directed to the pin, and for that to be possible the pin must be an object of consciousness. That presupposes, to use the terminology that has become accepted since a revival of interest in Brentano, intentionality. Brentano[7] thought that mentality was determined by certain mental acts – those of representation, judgment and what he called 'the phenomena of love and hate' – each of which was to be thought of as directed to a certain kind of object. He revived, to describe that 'direction', the mediaeval notion of the intending or tendency of the mind to an object, and since in each case the object in question need not be a real object he characterised it as an intentional object and as one which had *in*-existence as related only to the act in question. Moreover, the so-called relation was not, in consequence, a real relation. Subsequent philosophers have perhaps paid more attention to the idea of the direction of consciousness to an object than to that object's inexistence. In a way the direction of consciousness is the more fundamental point although it is of some importance nevertheless that in the 'acts of mind' in question their supposed object need not exist or need not exist as it is taken to be. In feeling a pin sticking into one, to revert to my earlier example, there need be no actual pin sticking into one.

However, that may be, it is clear that in order for perception to involve belief about something that thing must be an object *for* the perceiver. For that to be possible the perceiver must be in the position to attend to it, but that will be possible only if in turn the thing is a possible object of consciousness for him or her. (Sometimes, it should be noted, something can be an object of consciousness for us, when our attention is not directed, or not wholly directed, to it.) When, in having a pain, we do feel a pin sticking in to us, the pain, which may or may not be the main thing attended to, determines the mode of consciousness involved. As I said in chapter 3, sensations give the perceptual experience the phenomenal character that it has, and their perspective, in terms of the bodily framework which makes them possible, adds to that character. Thus in feeling the pin sticking in to one, one is not only conscious of the pin in a certain way – by feeling, which involves bodily sensations – but in relation to a certain part of the body. Analogously, in seeing a given object one is conscious of it in a certain way – by sight, which involves visual experiences or sensations – but in relation to a framework or field of objects in which it is placed.[8] But the most important point for present purposes is that the object and the field in which it is perceived must both be objects of consciousness for us in a way that also makes it possible, though not necessary, for there to be beliefs about them.[9] Perceptual belief thus depends on consciousness of objects which has the phenomenal character it has because of the sensations which one is then having, and which, when the object has a physical existence, are produced causally by it. But belief must also presuppose concepts if it is to be *about* whatever is its object, and if the object is to be of a certain kind for the believer, and not just a bare object. That, however, is true not just of belief; it holds good of perceiving an object as such and such, which may not, as we have already seen in connection with illusions, entail believing it to be such and such. This is something to which we must next turn, but the fact that this is true of 'perceiving-as' indicates that belief has a natural connection with perception; it is not something that is just added to it as a matter of contingent fact.

Notes

1 Aristotle presents a difficult argument to the same end in *De Anima* III.3, 428a24ff. This has been well expounded by K. Lycos in (1964), 'Aristotle and Plato on appearing', *Mind* 73, pp.496ff., and he uses it to refute the arguments of D.M. Armstrong in favour of an analysis, albeit a complex analysis, of perception in terms of belief. But simpler arguments are available, as I have tried to indicate.

2 Cf. Close, D. (1976), 'What is non-epistemic seeing?', *Mind*, 85, pp.161–70, and Pappas, G.S., 'Seeing e and seeing n', ibid., pp.171–88.

3 Dretske, Fred (v), *Seeing and Knowing*, Routledge and Kegan Paul: London.

4 See e.g. the references given in n.2.

5 See on this my (1977), 'The concept of information in Gibson's theory of perception', *Journal for the Theory of Social Behaviour*, 7, pp.5–16, reprinted in my (1983), *Perception, Learning and the Self*, Routledge and Kegan Paul: London, pp.30–42.

6 See the references given in chapter 2, n.6.

7 Brentano, Franz (1973), *Psychology from an Empirical Standpoint*, (1874), Kraus, Oskar (ed.), trans. Antos C. Rancurello, D.B. Terrell and Linda L. McAlister, Routledge and Kegan Paul: London.

8 The importance of the idea of phenomenal fields is emphasised by M. Merleau-Ponty in his (1962), *The Phenomenology of Perception*, trans. Colin Smith, Routledge and Kegan Paul: London.

9 Brentano thought that the mental acts that he distinguished and their intentional objects were hierarchically organised, so that those later in the series were dependent on those coming earlier. Whether that is correct in general need not be our concern here, though what I have been saying does support the thesis that judgment depends on presentation or representation. I have argued elsewhere that love and hate, however, do not presuppose any judgment or belief of a substantive kind. See my (1978), 'The phenomena of love and hate', *Philosophy*, 53, pp.5–20, reprinted in my *Perception, Learning and the Self*, pp.267–85.

Chapter 6
Perception and concepts – seeing-as

I noted in chapter 2 that some recent philosophers wish to argue that the content of perception is either to some extent or always non-conceptual.[1] The most extreme version of that view involves the claim that it is belief alone that is the place for conceptual content, if only because belief is propositional in form and one needs concepts to understand at least the descriptive aspect of propositions. A complete separation of belief from perception in this way makes it difficult to see how perception can give rise to beliefs except in a purely causal way that makes the idea of perceptual beliefs (i.e. beliefs formed actually in perceiving) more or less unintelligible. On the other hand, it seems undeniable that some of the complexities of our perceptions are not a matter of the complexities of our understanding. The complexities of the causal processes that give rise to perception and of what one might call our perceptual machinery (the structuring of our sense-organs and of the processes whereby they interact with whatever stimulates them when perception takes place) make their own contribution to the structure possessed by the forms that perception of the world may take. This is most obvious in connection with spatial perception, and this has led Christopher Peacocke to introduce the idea of perceptual scenarios, something that he thinks of as distinct from concepts.[2]

One needs to be careful here. Our sense-organs are themselves structured, and certain aspects of perception would not be possible if this were not so. Some features of the history of thinking about perception illustrate that point. The legacy of Humean ways of thinking combined with certain views of physiology (particularly the doctrine of specific nervous energies put forward by Johannes Müller in the 1830s) led to acceptance of the view that perceptual experience was punctiform. The question then arose how perception of continuously extended aspects of things was possible. One answer given to that question was that spatial perception, the perception of spatial relations, was a product of the temporal relations between the punctiform perceptions as they occur in succession. This view has a kind of absurdity about it and this is a product of the mistaken basis of the whole way of thinking – the idea that perceptions are ultimately punctiform, comprising what was termed a 'mosaic'.[3] On the other hand, it is also clear that we, and animals generally, sometimes react to spatial aspects of the world in a way that is unlearned and apparently unthinking. An animal can so react to an itch or other sensation in a part of its body; humans and animals can turn instinctively in the direction of a noise or a bright object in their field of vision. There is also the phenomenon of the visual cliff, in which a baby may show reluctance to crawl over a sheet of glass spread over an apparent drop (though it is less clear that this is an unlearned reaction, given that the baby is old enough to crawl). These are just some examples of reactions which one may not want to class as instances where something is perceived *as* such and such, but which are nevertheless reactions which would not be possible unless something about ones sensory apparatus made the spatial move possible. They are a function of structured sense-organs and structured sensory organisation.

In a way, this realisation is not new. Kant, who, historically speaking, is as much responsible as anyone for the idea that perception, in the form of perceptual judgments, depends on concept use, also thought that perception involves what he called 'intuitions' (*Anschauungen*) the form of which is spatio-temporal. Kant also thought that there were pure intuitions of space and time which were *apriori*, and so not derived from experience. But that would not be possible if experience itself, whatever it comprised an intuition *of*, did not have a form which was in some sense spatio-temporal. I say 'in some sense' because experiences themselves are not literally spatial (even if they have a temporal aspect); nevertheless what they are *of* is certainly and necessarily spatial. Unfortunately, Kant inherited and accepted the view that we are 'given' impressions (what he called presentations or representations – *Vorstellungen*) and he did not for that reason distinguish clearly between experiences and what experiences are of, or indeed between sensation and perception. (Schopenhauer criticised him on the first point, but accused him not of insufficient realism in his theory of perception, but of insufficient idealism!) One might put Kant's thought in other words, however, by saying that in his view perception has dual content, corresponding to the matter and form of the perceptions themselves (the matter being what they are of, the form being their spatio-temporal character). The spatio-temporal form is a 'given' and thus in a sense *apriori* in that it does not comprise a content derived from experience in the way that empirical concepts have to be derived.

The structured aspects of perception are thus the result of our perceptual organisation (for they would not be possible unless our sensory apparatus was organised in the way that it is). They might, as I have said, be held to give perception a content which is independent of concepts. Indeed they in many ways provide the framework for concept use and application. One must not, however, confuse that framework with what it is applied to. The fact that our sensory apparatus is organised in a structured way so that our perceptual experience is also structured does not mean that we do not have to employ concepts, and a concept of space in particular, in spatial perception. For spatial relations hold good of objects in the world, and we have to learn what it is for objects to be so related – to be behind each other, to the left or right and so on. Only when we have so learned what it is for objects to be spatially related can we perceive them as such. Indeed one could not perceive them as spatial at all in any adequate sense unless we had that understanding. Sensations may have what F.H. Bradley called 'voluminousness' in being distributed in a quasi-spatial way, and this too is a function of the organisation of our sensory apparatus. But this feature of sensations must not be confused with the spatial character of the objects of perception, any more than sensation should be confused with perception itself.4

It follows from all this that if it is true that perception involves non-conceptual content it does so in the sense that perception is naturally structured by what makes it possible. Moreover, some reactions which are equally to be explained by what makes it possible need not be thought of as perceptual at all, as I have indicated. Peacocke's 'scenarios' are merely the frameworks for our perception of the world in this way. They are far from being all that there is to it and they do not obviate the fact that what fills in that framework has to be learnt through the application of concepts to things in experience. It is the latter which supplies the major form of content to perception. The way in which this works can be seen by considering what it is to see things *as* such and such, something that might be thought to be analogous to judging them to be such and such, but which, as we saw earlier in considering illusions like the Müller-Lyer, do not amount to judgment if that is the same as belief. If it is claimed, as it sometimes is, that it is belief that is the proper place for concept use, the phenomena of seeing-as belie that claim.

As far as seeing-as is concerned one needs again to go carefully. There are at least two sorts of cases in which it is appropriate to say that one is seeing something as such and such, one of which has gained a sort of notoriety as a result of Wittgenstein's remarks on seeing aspects in his *Philosophical Investigations* II.xi.5 This is the sort of seeing-as which is imaginative. It is perhaps typified, as it is in Wittgenstein's remarks, by those cases in which we see something as a representation of something else, particularly in the example of ambiguous figures. I shall leave consideration of this until the next chapter. The other, more straightforward, kind of seeing-as, which I shall be concerned with now, is correlative with looks or appearances. It is the sort of case in which one simply sees something as a tree or as green. The only question perhaps is whether, as with looks or appearances, it is true that whenever one sees something one sees it as such and such. (Is it the case that whenever one sees something it looks such and such to one?) Is all seeing seeing-as? Is all perceiving perceiving-as?

It is clear enough that it can be said of me that I have seen something without my having seen it as anything. But then it can be said of me that I have seen something without my having been aware of seeing anything at all. Hence it might be argued that in those cases where I can be said to have seen something without seeing it as anything it is because I was not aware of seeing anything at all, and *a fortiori* was not aware of seeing it *as* anything. Otherwise, I must surely have seen it as whatever it is. It is probably unprofitable to go further into such considerations. The fact remains that in the normal case if I see something I must see it as something or other. I say 'something or other' advisedly. That something or other may be a matter of the thing's characterisation, the properties it is seen to have, but it may be a matter simply of its identification, what it is; and I can surely see something as, say, an elephant, without *seeing* what properties it has, even if I know anyway that, being an elephant, it must have such and such properties. But an elephant is in any case a complex object and in more simple objects (even if there is nothing which is absolutely simple) the situation seems even more obvious; I can see a colour, red, without even being in the position, because of the circumstances in which I see it, to see it as a red of a certain shade or saturation. Nevertheless, I must still see it as red.

If I do see it, or something, as red, this can only be because, given the other things that contribute to my having the experience that I have, it looks that way. But it can do that only if also I know something about colour and about red in particular. That knowledge will not of itself make it look that way, but neither will the causal circumstances or the sensations produced by them do that. This is obvious in the case of tactual or bodily perception; some form of pressure on the skin producing a certain kind of sensation is not enough to ensure that the object feels sharp or blunt unless one knows what sharpness or bluntness in things is. It might be objected that in these circumstances the object must at least feel something or other. But that is not so unless one knows already what it is for there to be an object of feeling, and this entails the intentionality referred to in the previous chapter. One must already have come, however that happens, to consciousness of a world of objects which can be related in various ways to oneself.

On the other hand, sometimes something can come to look quite different as a result of the recognition that it is of a certain kind or has a certain kind of properties. Things, we sometimes say, click into place in this way. It has even been claimed by Irvin Rock[6] that when people are got to wear inverting spectacles or prisms, which makes things look initially the wrong way up, it can eventually happen that things come to look, as a result of what is called 'perceptual adaptation', the right way up. There are perhaps some problems about how 'look' is to be interpreted in these cases, but the claims, in some sense or other, seem undeniable. There are in any case many quite familiar cases of things coming to look quite different as the result of some form of learning, and while not all these are simply a matter of the application of knowledge in recognition, some of them are just that. In such cases it is the knowledge that the thing in question is whatever it is that makes it suddenly come to look that way. It would be a mistake to suggest that in the circumstances knowledge overcomes the causal processes which make the thing initially look otherwise; for those causal processes still hold good. In any case there are circumstances in which no amount of knowledge by itself makes any difference, as we saw earlier in connection with the Müller-Lyer illusion. For in that illusion the lines look of different length in spite of the fact that we know otherwise, and if we are able to get them to look of the same length it is by, for example, so attending to the lines that we are able to ignore the effect of the arrow-heads. Similarly, in ambiguous figures, such as the duck-rabbit figure invented by Jastrow and made notorious among philosophers by Wittgenstein's discussion in his *Philosophical Investigations* II.xi, we can sometimes produce a shift of aspect by concentration on one feature of the figure, but not just by anything that we know about the figure. If that is true in general, it is true in particular in relation to that form of knowledge that is involved in having a concept of, or applicable to, the thing in question.

What makes the thing come to look different in those cases where we are inclined to say that this is the product of a recognition of the thing's identity or character is not simply knowledge but a knowledge that is seen as having application in the case in question. The point is connected with what Kant, in the section of the *Critique of Pure Reason* having that title, called the doctrine of the schematism.[7] Kant had a profound insight into the problem in question here, although his own solution has often been regarded as being rather obscure. What Kant saw was that it is at least theoretically possible to have the concept of a dog, to know what dogs are, without being able to recognise any actual dogs. Some philosophers want, in an opposite spirit, to analyse concept-possession, purely in terms of recognitional powers, but it is clearly possible to recognise all and only dogs but not *as* dogs. To recognise dogs as dogs one needs more than a recognitional power manifested purely in discriminative behaviour. But in that case the problem arises of the connection between the possibly abstract knowledge of what dogs are and that discriminative behaviour, and even between the abstract knowledge and the perceptual recognition. Concepts vary, as I shall indicate directly, in their abstract character and thereby in their closeness to their possible concrete applications in perception, but the problem is there throughout.

Kant said that to make the connection that is requisite there is needed what he called a 'schema', which somehow sets out the applications of the abstract concept. He said that this had something to do with the imagination and was due to a power buried in the depths of the human soul – a way of putting it that may suggest that it is just a mystery. It is indeed a mystery, but not just a mystery. A philosopher who was straightforwardly empiricist might say that there is no mystery here at all; our concepts are ultimately derived from experience, so that there need be no surprise that they get application to things in experience. The problem seems to arise because the connection with experience in the case of some concepts is indirect or at least complex. What we understand in having the concept of a dog may involve, for example, an understanding, at least to some extent, of biological systems of classification, but these get application to experience via the more obviously experiential properties that dogs have. There is not the same problem in the case of, say, the concept of red, which is directly and obviously connected with experience, and there is no need to postulate a general connecting link between concepts and perception of the kind that Kant's doctrine of the schematism seems to want.

Such a view is, however, a snare and a delusion. The concept of red is not derived directly from experience (nor is any concept), although it is quite true that we need experience, indeed visual experience, to have a full understanding of what red is. I say 'full understanding' because it is not true that blind people can have no understanding at all of colour. A blind man can know that red is, for example, more similar to orange than it is to blue, and there is some understanding exhibited by Locke's man who thought that scarlet was like the sound of a trumpet. This is because even simple concepts such as that of red presuppose structural considerations. Colours do not stand by themselves, nor could they; they have relations to each other, which can be set out in such constructions as the so-called colour circle, whether or not that does justice to all the aspects of colour. But it is true that in the understanding of colour the place of experience and thereby of recognitional considerations looms large, so that the possibility of understanding the concept red but not being able to recognise red things is much more remote than is the case with the concept of a dog. Nevertheless, the structural considerations which I have mentioned still have to be linked in understanding with the experience of the single colour. There are other considerations of an analogous kind too, such as require an understanding of what kinds of things can have colour.8

Nevertheless, there are certainly differences, as suggested earlier, between the ways in which different concepts are related to experience. As far as concerns the forms of perception involved and their relation to objects we owe more to Aristotle than we do to later empiricist philosophers. For Aristotle distinguished between different objects of the senses – special, common and incidental – in terms of the relation that exists between the definition of the sense and that of the object. Sight, he said, is related to colour and hearing to sound in that the definition of the sense makes reference to the object, or perhaps vice versa.9 But shape and size are perceptible by more than one sense-organ; they are in that sense common perceptibles (and, Aristotle thinks, they are essential objects of a common sense, as colour is of the special sense, vision). By contrast, there is no essential connection between any form of perception and the identity of an object, even a perceptible object. When, to use Aristotle's example, we see the son of Cleon, the whiteness which we perceive is essentially a visual property, and his shape is essentially a property perceptible by a sense common to the organs of sight and touch; but his identity is not essentially a perceptible property at all. It just happens, incidentally, that the white, peculiarly shaped, object is the son of Cleon. This does not mean that it is wrong to suggest that we see the son of Cleon or see him *as* the son of Cleon; it is just that being the son of Cleon is not essentially a matter of perception.

Whether or not it is helpful to put these matters in the way in which Aristotle puts them, and whether or not his precise claims are true, it seems clear that the concept of a colour demands for its full understanding some form of visual experience, and the concept of, say, shape similarly demands for its full understanding some form of either visual or tactual experience (and arguably both), while many other concepts demand nothing of the kind. Hence one can see why there might be thought to be a gap to be crossed between having the concept of a dog and being able to have the perceptual recognition of a dog. For while a dog may have properties the understanding of which has a close connection with

44

perception, the property of being a dog does not have such a close connection. The property of being white has a much closer connection in that a full understanding of what it is for something to be white demands visual experience, just as a full understanding of what it is for something to be of a certain shape demands either visual or tactual experience (and arguably both). Nevertheless, the gap is not thereby removed altogether, for in order to make the essential connection in these cases I have had to speak of *full* understanding. Having a concept is not an all or none matter, and the form of knowledge involved in it – knowing what it is for something to be X – can be a matter of degree. That is why it is reasonable to say that a blind man can have *some* understanding of what it is for something to be white or red, and thus to have *to some extent* the concepts in question.

What this all means is that there are always in effect two components in seeing something as such and such – the experiential and the conceptual. The fact that these necessarily come together in the seeing-as does not belie that fact that the knowledge involved in the conceptual component may vary in its degree of abstraction and thus in the closeness of its connection with the experiential component. But there is never an identity between the two, so that there is always in theory, if not in practice, a gap to be crossed. To say, as Kant does, that this is a function of the imagination is simply to say that formal or abstract knowledge needs to be cashed in concrete terms and that this happens in perception in a way which is similar to the way in which such knowledge can be cashed in terms of images when one imagines something. (For there is a parallel problem in the case of imagining concerning the extent to which the imagining presupposes the application of knowledge that one already has and just how an image functions in this respect.) The important thing about seeing-as, as I said earlier, is that the knowledge involved is not simply knowledge but a knowledge seen as having application to the case in question, and if there is a problem it is one about how this is to be conceived as possible.

I said that the knowledge in question is *seen* as having application to the case in question. This might suggest that I am trying to explain one case of seeing as – the seeing of the object as a such and such – by another – the seeing of a form of knowledge as having application to the case in question. That, however, is not what I have in mind. The point is that it is not enough in order to see something as a dog to know what dogs are and see the thing in question. It not even enough to know that a dog is an X which is F and G and to see the thing in question as an X which is F and G; it is arguably not even enough to know that this thing is a dog and to see it as an X which is F and G. To see something as a dog what one knows about dogs in general and in particular must be given application to the thing *in perception*; it must be *seen* as having this application. There are indeed cases in which one may know exactly what something is but just cannot see it as that. The 'click', so to speak, that occurs when it falls into place perceptually is well known; and then sometimes one finds it difficult to know how one can have failed to see it like that. Moreover, such cases are not always ones of straightforward recognition, such as that which came to Electra and Orestes, where the recogniser comes to see *that* the thing or person is what or who it, he or she is. Nor is the seeing-as necessarily of that perhaps peculiar kind in which one may see something as F, without it's looking F, because in speaking of seeing-as here one is registering a form of perceptual belief, parallel to the perceptual knowledge that one indicates in speaking of seeing-that.[10]

The 'click' of something falling into place perceptually is thus not a click of recognition in the ordinary sense. In it one instance of seeing-as is transformed into another. Perhaps the most obvious examples of this are those involved in the seeing of ambiguous figures, like the 'duck/rabbit', referred to earlier. In such examples there is, to use Wittgenstein's terminology, the dawning of an aspect, most often in such a way that the aspect that previously dominated the perception is abolished. What was previously a clear example of a picture of a duck becomes equally clearly a picture of a rabbit. (This is what occurs most often although I do not think that the possibility of something looking as both an X and a Y can be excluded; indeed there are some perceptual experiences in which one can describe what one sees adequately only by saying that whatever one sees both looks F and looks the contrary of F – which is not of course to say that it actually *is* both F and the contrary of F.[11] The 'duck/rabbit' is not a duck-rabbit, a picture of something that is both a duck and a rabbit, but it may look both, certainly successively and perhaps at the same time.) One can sometimes learn to control such aspect-dawnings, by, say, concentrating one's attention on some aspect of the object as opposed to another. But there is no possibility of that in the duck/rabbit case if one knows nothing of ducks or rabbits, and without some relevant knowledge an aspect will not dawn at all. In transferring one's attention in the way suggested one is in effect manipulating some of the causal conditions of the perception, but the role of attention here and in perception in general is something to which I shall return in chapter 10.

For the moment, however, it may be useful to consider how a concentration of one's attention on one feature of the thing or picture (say, the curve which can be seen as the mouth of the rabbit) can make it look one thing, the rabbit, rather than the other. I have said that it involves a manipulation of the causal conditions of the perception. It does that in this case by enabling the picture to be structured in one way rather than another (as, say, right-facing, rather than left-facing, and so as having one particular orientation). It may not be able to be seen as a rabbit without being seen as so structured, although it cannot be seen as a rabbit at all without some knowledge of what rabbits are like. (Or, to be more accurate, one must at least believe that rabbits are such and such, and belief of that kind presupposes some relevant knowledge.) If one does see it as a rabbit by so structuring what is there to be seen in a certain way in one's perception, all that is a matter of seeing-as. It is not the thing itself that is so structured; it is rather one's view of it that is so affected. Then when the aspect dawns, there is what Wittgenstein describes as 'the echo of a thought in sight' (p.212e). (And that is just one of the many wise things that he has to say about seeing-as in this section of the *Philosophical Investigations*.)

It is the *echo* of a thought because it is not thinking full-blown. As Wittgenstein remarks about being struck by an impression of something (p.211e), this is not looking (*Schauen*) *plus* thinking. The thought, that is to say the concept, is not just added to something else in seeing-as. The phenomenon, the experience, is already conceptually imbued, as one might put it. That is why I have had to emphasise that when one sees something as F the knowledge that is involved in having the concept of F has to be *seen* as applying to the case in question; it is not simply added to the sensory experience which is caused by the object perceived, however that is structured. If one remains with a sense of mystery about seeing-as, when it has been thoroughly discussed, this may be only because seeing-as cannot be analysed into distinct components, which are then added together. Imaginative seeing-as, to which I shall now turn, reinforces that point.

Notes

1 For references see chapter 2, note 6. The underlying motive for accepting the view is derived from theories of information processing to be found in cognitive science.

2 See e.g. his 'Scenarios, concepts and perception' in Crane, Tim (ed.) (1992), *The Contents of Experience: Essays on Perception*, CUP: Cambridge.

3 For some details of this see my (1961), *Sensation and Perception*, Routledge and Kegan Paul: London, chapter 8. Gestalt psychology was part of the reaction that occurred to this way of thinking.

4 See my (1990), *In and Out of the Black Box*, Blackwell: Oxford, pp.89–91, where I criticise in these terms the claims made by Marr in his theory of perception for the computation of spatial characteristics on the basis of what he calls the 'primal sketch' provided by perceptual mechanisms. His claim is based on what happens when random-dot stereograms are presented to the eyes in such a way as to produce retinal disparity; one part of the pattern may appear to float in front of another. Retinal disparity has traditionally been set down as one of the 'cues' for space-perception; but it is no more than one of the things which is a condition of its possibility, it does not, without reference to a concept of space, explain space perception.

5 Wittgenstein, L. (1953), *Philosophical Investigations*, Blackwell: Oxford, pp.193ff.

6 See e.g. Rock, Irvin (1966), *The Nature of Perceptual Adaptation*, Basic Books Inc.: New York and London.

7 See also Strawson, P.F. (1974), 'Imagination and perception' in his *Freedom and Resentment*, Methuen: London, pp.45–654.

8 Distinctions have for example been drawn between surface and film colours – between the kinds of colour and the kinds of experience appropriate to them which pertain to the surfaces of solid objects (whether or not the colours in question carry on inside them) and those which pertain to liquids or gases, where

the colour certainly looks to extend right through the volume occupied by the liquid or gas.

9 See the discussion in my (1968), *Aristotle's De Anima II and III*, Clarendon Press: Oxford, of *De Anima*, II. 6, III. 1 (pp.105ff., 117ff.) and Sorabji, R. 'Aristotle on demarcating the five senses', *Phil. Rev.*, 80, pp.55–79, reprinted in Barnes, J., Schofield, M. and Sorabji, R. (eds.) (1979), *Articles on Aristotle*, Vol. 4, Duckworth: London, pp.76–92. See also my Inaugural Lecture at Birkbeck College, London, 'Seeing things as they are', reprinted in part in my *The Psychology of Perception*, Routledge and Kegan Paul: London, 1969 version only).

10 I owe the recognition of this kind of seeing-as to Mr. Clifford Lill. It is arguable, however, that a similar distinction has to be made in connection with 'looks', and this has been maintained by e.g. Roderick Chisholm in his (1957), *Perceiving*, Cornell U.P.: Ithaca, New York. The point is that sometimes, but not always, to say that something looks F or looks to be F is to say how, so to speak, one finds it as a result of perception. That is a matter of one's beliefs, generated by perception, but not all looks are like that. One might, in the case of the Müller-Lyer illusion say, almost paradoxically, that the lines look of different length, though to me, since I am very familiar with the illusion, they look of the same length. Do things seen from the top of a tall building look small? Does a straight stick in water look bent? Yes and no. It certainly looks as a straight stick in water looks, as J.L. Austin insisted in his (1962), *Sense and Sensibilia*, Clarendon Press: Oxford.

11 Tim Crane has invoked the so-called 'waterfall illusion' in this connection; after looking at a waterfall for some time something else that is then seen may look both stationary and moving. See his (1988), 'The waterfall illusion', *Analysis*, 48, pp.142ff. Analogous phenomena are the experience of the rotating trapezoid demonstrated by Adelbert Ames Jr. (See my (1957), *The Psychology of Perception*, Routledge and Kegan Paul: London, p.103) and perhaps the experience of 'impossible objects' invoked by Richard Gregory. (See his 'Choosing a paradigm for perception' in Carterette, E.C. and Friedman, M.P. (eds.) (1974), *Handbook of Perception*, Academic Press: New York and London, pp.255–73, esp. pp.264–5.)

Chapter 7
Perception and the imagination –
seeing-as continued

Wittgenstein says in one much discussed passage in his *Philosophical Investigations* II.xi (p.213e) that 'The concept of an aspect is akin to the concept of an image'. This has sometimes been taken as a comment on images, to the effect that the nature and role of an image can be elucidated in terms of seeing-as, so that having an image of X can be regarded as like seeing something as X without there actually being an X.[1] It seems fairly clear, however, from what Wittgenstein goes on to say that he intends it the other way round (although the English translation is arguably somewhat tendentious in translating ' *Vorstellung*' as 'image'). For he says 'In other words: the concept "I am now seeing it as ...." is akin to "I am now having *this* image"'; and he goes on to ask whether it does not need imagination (*Phantasie*)to hear something as a variation on a particular theme, though the hearing is clearly a form of perception (I shall return to this example or ones like it later.) Seeing-as of this kind, or at any rate of the kind involved in the 'duck/rabbit', he says earlier (p.197e), and perhaps confusingly, is not part of perception, 'and for that reason it is like seeing and again not like'. For seeing the duck/rabbit as a rabbit is not the same as, and perhaps not even very like, seeing a rabbit or even seeing a straightforward picture of a rabbit. The duck/rabbit figure is a representation in being a figure, but it is not an ordinary or straightforward representation of either a duck or a rabbit. One might indeed say, as he suggests about a different example on p.193e that the seeing-as involves interpretation, but it is not clear that we should say that about a straightforward picture of a rabbit. So the sense in which the concept of an aspect is akin to the concept of an image is that it takes imagination to see it that way, whereas it does not take imagination in the same way to see something as a rabbit (not in ordinary circumstances at any rate).

I say that it does not take imagination *in the same way* to see something as a rabbit, because, it will be remembered, Kant argued that imagination is involved even in that case, to enable a concept to be given application to an instance in perception. However, in the cases with which we are now concerned the perception can be said to be truly imaginative, and one would not usually say that about ordinary perception. Roger Scruton has tried to make the point by connecting imaginative seeing-as with the quasi-Fregean notion of an unasserted thought. 2 The idea is that in imaginative seeing one brings to bear a thought about the object without any suggestion that it is being asserted that that is how the object actually is. In that way one might see an ember in the fire as a certain object or a cloud as, say, a face, and in such imaginative seeing the imagination is, one might say, free.3 The trouble with this thesis is that imaginative seeing so construed seems to have a place mostly, if not entirely, in those cases where there is, so to speak, a certain ambiguity in the object of perception; that is to say that the object is such that there is room for its being taken in more than one way, and it does not have a single, fixed, identity. (And in works of representational art that must always be the case because of the distinction in their case between the medium of representation and their representational role.) But the imagination can have a place too in enabling us to see how things actually are, so that in seeing them as such and such the seeing-as then comes to involve a thought which is not just unasserted.

One might indeed say that the seeing-as which involves an unasserted thought is parasitical on the seeing-as which involves a quasi-assertion. This is because one cannot arrange in the mind's eye, so to speak, what is there without at least being in the position to see what is there in another way, without this being a matter of arrangement in the mind's eye. In the latter case, if one does see what is there in that way, it will not be a matter of a thought merely entertained; to see it in that way will be to represent it to oneself in that way, whether or not believingly. However that may be, when the object is sufficiently complicated, seeing what it is may well demand arranging its elements in the mind's eye, paying, perhaps, more attention to some elements than to others. Perhaps only then will the object's identity really emerge. That is how it often is with puzzle pictures. The more one is content with what immediately presents itself to one's sight the less will one be able to see what is actually there.

This use of the imagination is not the 'Kantian' one involved in what he calls the schematism. It is not just a matter of bringing something under a suitable concept; it is a matter of seeing how this is even possible, when it does not immediately look like that. Once the task is accomplished it may seem obvious that that is how it is, but the exercise *may* have to be gone through again the next time one is confronted with the object in question. That is certainly how it characteristically is with puzzle pictures or with ambiguous figures in which one aspect seems to be more obvious than the other. It is how it is also with some Cubist pictures, where the arrangement of parts of the body which are represented may not be the natural one. To see a limb in that case as what it is and in some functional relation to other parts of the body represented clearly demands imagination, even when the depiction of the limb by itself is more or less naturalistic. The latter holds, for example, when, as is sometimes the case, Picasso represents an eye set in a face's profile as how it looks from the front. This does not always look unnatural at first sight, because it is an obvious eye and is where an eye should be. But its functional misplacement has to be overcome when that is noticed, and only the imagination can bring that about.

The objects of perception in which these uses of the imagination arise are complex. Another use of the imagination is to enable something simple to be given a wider context. An example of Wittgenstein's is pertinent here. This is the example of a simple right-angled triangle with the right-angle at the top which, as Wittgenstein points out (p.200e) can be seen 'as a triangular hole, as a solid, as a geometrical drawing; as standing on its base, as hanging from its apex; as a mountain, as a wedge, as an arrow or pointer, as an overturned object which is meant to stand on the shorter side of the right-angle, as a half parallelogram, and as various other things.' To see the triangle in one of these ways is to see it as more than it immediately presents itself as being, and it is noteworthy that this is not always a matter of seeing it as a representation of something; one can see it itself as more than a mere collection of lines on paper. One can similarly see a physical object as more than is immediately apparent; I might, for example, see the tree facing me at the opposite side of my garden as a menacing giant, with arms outstretched. To do so is certainly to phantasise, but not in the sense of making play with images. In so seeing the tree I am certainly *seeing* it as the thing in question. Moreover, while this may involve, as I said earlier, a free use of the imagination, the imaginative seeing may in other circumstances be, so to speak, forced upon one by the circumstances in which the perception takes place. (It may be more likely, for example, when the illumination is not good or when one is in a certain mood.)

In these kinds of case the imagination supplies a context, a way of seeing which is not literal (which is not at all to say that it is unnatural). Let us, however, return to the cases where that context is supplied for us, but in which the imagination plays a role. I mentioned earlier Wittgenstein's remark about it requiring imagination to hear something as a variation on a particular theme. The same may hold good of seeing family resemblances, another notion with which Wittgenstein had much to do. To see a child as like his or her father or grandmother, one has to concentrate on certain aspects of the child's appearance to the exclusion of others, and it may be that this is something that some people can do while others cannot (just as some people may find an insuperable difficulty in imagining being a tree, while others do not). A composer who presents a set of variations on a theme is trying to preserve something as constant throughout the variations while shrouding that in a changing context and set of forms. Moreover, the interaction between what is constant and what is variable must not be too obvious, so that the ingenuity and creativity of the variations as a work of art have to depend upon the way in which the imagination is stimulated by them. But it is essential that what is constant can be heard as such within the changing context.

It might perhaps be said that, since a piece of music like a set of variations takes place over time, hearing the sections as variations on a theme is essentially a memory phenomenon and not specifically a perceptual one. But that is not so. It is not to be disputed that memory enters into the phenomenon, but hearing (or for that matter seeing, ...) something as the one which one heard before does not require imagination. Much of perception involves memory in one way or another, to the extent that what one perceives now is or is connected with what one perceived before (though it is worth noting that regarding a form of perception as in some way a function of the past is not in itself to regard it as a memory phenomenon – the past can affect one's present perception in other ways than through memory[4]). But perceiving something as the one which one perceived before does not of itself require any imaginative feat, merely memory and recognition. It is another matter if what one perceives now is connected in some more subtle way with what one perceived before; the relationship between the different perceptions must in that case have a certain complexity which requires an unpacking and reconstruction in the imagination.

There may indeed be argument in the case of some forms of perception which seem imaginative whether that complexity is there. Wine tasters are sometimes accused of excessive use of the imagination in their descriptions of the taste of wine (and the same applies to perfumes). Surely, it might be said, the taste of a wine is not complicated enough for this to be a genuine use of the imagination in perception; in this case the imagination surely goes beyond anything that is genuinely perceptual. But these descriptions of taste generally depend on analogies, and for an analogy to hold there must be similarity along more than one dimension. In fact a taste may have more complexity than is recognised at first, and nothing then in principle stands in the way of the claim that tasting the wine as such and such may be both reasonable and imaginative, whether or not the description offered is in fact right or even illuminating.

Imagination entails either rearrangement of elements in a complicated situation or putting what is simple in a complex thought structure so that what at first appears simple can be seen as potentially more complex through its context. That may be so even if that complexity is merely a matter of the relations of the thing in question to other objects, especially relations of similarity and difference. One might note in this connection what is involved in hearing some kinds of music, especially perhaps some of the compositions of Anton Webern, in which, as it is sometimes said, a note may stand out like a jewel. The note may be thought to shine out simply because of its isolation, but because its jewel-like characteristics do in fact depend on its context. In the sort of case in question the context is presented over time according to a potentially recognisable principle, however difficult it may be for some, too used to tonal music, to hear the principle inherent in the tone-row. But in this instance the principle constitutes a given; it take a much greater feat of imagination, and one which more nearly borders on phantasy, to construct the context for oneself. The same applies, perhaps to a lesser extent, to hearing an allusion in music, an emotionally inspired thought perhaps, which is not derived from any obvious principle, however much some musical theorists, such as Deryck Cooke have thought to find in music natural principles akin to those which govern language.

52

It is important, however, that what I have been talking about is not just phantasy in the sense of allowing the mind to range over various possibilities in regard to an object. What I have been talking about is, however imaginative, perception in a genuine sense. In the ordinary cases of seeing-as where there is a straightforward kind of concept use, the thought that is implicit in the perception may or may not be obvious either to oneself or to others. It may be argued, as Kant and Strawson have done, that the fact that there is a kind of gap between the concept and its application in perception is enough to make the perception a function of the imagination. But that gap does not of itself constitute the kind of complexity and sometimes ambiguity that I have been indicating as present in the objects of really imaginative perception. To see a figure as a triangle is very different from seeing it in one of the ways which Wittgenstein lists in the quotation given earlier.

Sometimes, of course, the imaginative seeing may be thought by others extravagant. He is reading too much into the situation, they may say. Certainly one's imagination may sometimes take over, so to speak, so that the suggestion that one is seeing whatever is there as such and such can be set down as a form of delusion on one's part. A delusion, however, is normally a defect of belief or set of beliefs. The suggestion, therefore, that an extravagantly imaginative way of seeing things is a delusion has the implication that the use of the imagination has so taken over as to affect beliefs. It undermines a just sense of reality, we might say. For, apart from the fact that over-imaginativeness may affect beliefs, there can be nothing wrong with it, considered simply as a feat of imagination. To suppose otherwise would be to put undue restrictions on artistic license, as it is called. If I insist on seeing the tree in my garden as a giant with arms outstretched, that is all right as long as it is still imagination and I recognise that it is so. If it affects my everyday life it will be because the imagination has altered my beliefs in some way. (It is then a delusion, but not an illusion or hallucination. Illusions are partial errors in seeing, however they are produced; hallucinations are phenomena in which one seems to see something which is not there at all. It might be suggested that in seeing the tree as a giant in such a fixed way I do seem to see something that is not there – a giant; but there *is* something there, the tree, it is the way of seeing it which is wrong or at least extravagant.)

This sort of example also brings up another feature of seeing-as – the way in which it may be connected with emotional factors. Emotions, as distinct from mere moods, have objects and because of that entail a way of seeing them. Indeed the emotion may sometimes dictate the way of seeing. That might be true of a persistent tendency to see the tree as a giant, particularly if I see it as threatening in some way. Others might say that I would not see it in that way were not I emotionally inclined so to do. I shall not elaborate this sort of point further here. The underlying point is simply that it is not surprising to find a way of seeing things explicable in terms of emotional factors; for emotion itself generally entails seeing things in ways which are characteristic of that emotion. Someone who is emotionally constrained to see something in a way that affects his or her life in ways which are debilitating may have to learn to see that thing in a different way.

Whether or not that learning can take place without all sorts of other things being altered too does not affect the general point. I have spoken of learning to see things on previous occasions, and I shall return to the subject in order to expand on those remarks in the next chapter.

Notes

1 See e.g. Ishiguro, Hidé (1967), 'Imagination', *PASS*, 41, pp.37–56.
2 Scruton, Roger (1974), *Art and Imagination*, Methuen: London, Part II.
3 This is particularly true of what might be called 'seeing-in', which might be suggested as a better way of describing what is involved in the perception of pictures than 'seeing-as'. For it is not clear that it is really right to say that when one is confronted with a portrait of X one sees it (and what is the 'it' here?) *as* X. I believe, but I am not sure, that I owe something to Richard Wollheim here.
4 See my (1990), *In and Out of the Black Box*, Blackwell: Oxford, chapter 6, 'The Effect of the Past'.

Changes in ways of perceiving things can be brought about by various factors and in various ways. The changes may be due to factors in the causal conditions of perception – the illumination, the condition of the background, our physical relation to the thing in question, and so on. They may be due to something in ourselves – our conceptual understanding and changes in that, or even aspects of our emotional or volitional states. (We sometimes see what we want to see, or in some cases, paradoxically perhaps, what we do not want to see.)[1] Not all changes of that kind amount to learning, however. Indeed, some such changes may counteract the ways in which we have learnt to perceive the world, in the sense that, as with illusions in general, the ways of perceiving do not correspond to what we have learnt to be the correct way of seeing things. It would not be quite right, however, to maintain that learning always and only takes place in connection with what is the correct way of seeing things. We can learn not only to see things as they are, but, in what are perhaps less usual circumstances, to see things as they are not. That is to say that some illusions may themselves be the product of learning, or at any rate that learning figures in perceiving things in what would ordinarily be thought to be an illusory way.

There might be thought to be a certain perversity about the latter situation. But it is in some ways analogous to the learning of bad habits or incorrect ways of doing things (particularly in the context of skills). Just as someone might in certain circumstances get a certain pleasure from doing things in the 'wrong way', so someone might get pleasure from seeing things in the 'wrong way', and I am sure that there are many who react to recent forms of art in that way, rightly or not. If, however, it is right to say that someone is getting pleasure from a certain way of seeing things, it is also plausible to say that he or she must be adopting something like a technique in order to see them in that way. (That is not to say, of course, that it is impossible to get pleasure from a way of seeing things that is produced by quite external factors. Quite the contrary. But there is a difference between seeing something in a certain way that happens to produce pleasure and taking pleasure in seeing things in certain ways when this is the product of an activity of ours which is part of a learning process. For learning does seem to involve more on our part than is involved in purely causal processes, such as take place in conditioning.)[2]

However all that may be, when we consider that learning has played a part in a way of perceiving things we have entered into considerations which go beyond those which have to do with a concern simply with the causal conditions of perception, however much such causal factors may continue to play a role. Moreover, the fact that the causal aspects of perception are perhaps the most obvious has, arguably, underlaid the impetus towards a causal theory of perception in the sort of form discussed in chapter 4, and has led to an underestimation both of the part that learning plays in perception and of the extent to which perception is an active process.[3] I shall discuss the latter in the next chapter; here I shall concentrate on learning, whether or not active. Paradigmatically perhaps learning involves the acquisition of new knowledge or understanding through experience. Such knowledge may be either theoretical or practical (as is the case in skills, which must involve understanding at some point if they are to be differentiated from mere knacks – knowing how to do something is more than simply being able to do it). To the extent that perception can be regarded as a way of getting knowledge of the world, one might understand the part played by learning in that paradigmatic form.

But, as we have seen, that is not all that there is to perception, and there are clear ways in which learning can affect the actual perceptual experience. That is not to say that knowledge and understanding do not come into the picture somewhere and somehow; it is to say rather that knowledge and understanding may not be the end-product or goal of the process of perceptual learning. As the result of experience one may come to see things in a way in which we have not previously seen them. This will constitute learning if in that process the final way of seeing things is in some way *grounded* on that experience, and is not just a result of a purely causal process. In using the notion of a ground here I do not mean to suggest that the way of seeing things is the result of an inference from anything in that experience. The notion of inference has been invoked from time to time by theorists writing about perception, particularly Helmholtz, and because such inferences are not generally evident to the perceiver they have been deemed unconscious. It would be wrong to suggest that the notion of inference never has a part to play in a theory of perception, but as far as concerns perceptual experience itself the idea is problematic. This can be seen by considering one phenomenon in relation to which Helmholtz invoked the idea of unconscious inference – that of colour contrast.[4]

A grey patch seen in the middle of a red area will tend to look green because of the contrast with the surrounding colour, however that works. Helmholtz thought that this is because we have a tendency to take the inset patch as being seen through the surrounding colour. The suggestion is thus that the surrounding colour should affect the inset patch in the way that seeing things through coloured spectacles may do (though, incidentally, may not always do). In that case the inset patch, if grey, should look red. But it does not; it looks green. Helmholtz's argument is that this must be because we infer, unconsciously, that the patch's real colour is not grey but one which is shifted towards the opposite of red. As a result of this inference it looks green. (Helmholtz used similar arguments to explain why things at a distance, for example, do not always look of the size one would expect on the basis of the optical facts, but nearer to their actual size.) There are many oddities about this argument, including the premiss from which it all starts – the suggestion that we take ourselves to be seeing the inset patch through the surrounding area. But the point on which it is perhaps most useful to concentrate is the final one – that the patch's looking green follows directly from the inference. When we infer that something in our experience is of a certain kind, it by no means follows that it will then look that way to us. Indeed, quite the contrary. We may then be led to say that we can now see that the thing in question is F, even though it looks G. Seeing that, as I have indicated on a previous occasion, is a form of knowing, but however much one may know about a given thing it does not follow that it will thereby look that way.

The situation in regard to Helmholtz is in fact complicated by what might be thought implicit in what I have just said – that there is a gap between the knowledge and the looks. He claimed categorically that no sensory process could be overriden by intellectual processes or by learning. But by the sensory processes in question he understood the having of sensations which are the result of strictly causal factors. In the colour contrast case, therefore, the situation ought to be⁵ in his view that in looking at the grey patch we do have sensations of grey, even if the patch looks green. Somehow those sensations cease to affect how the patch looks; we must be unaware of them so that they too are unconscious, as well as the inference. So the inference is of the form 'I am having sensations of grey; but in red illumination something that produces such sensations cannot be grey, but must be green; so it is green' – all of which is unconscious. But my argument about the gap between knowledge and looks is different from this. However much sensations or sensory aspects of perception affect the way in which things look, the fact, if it is one, that intellectual processes cannot override those sensations does not entail that they cannot affect the looks. It is clear, for example, that how one conceives things may affect how they look to one. But that is not to say that what one knows or believes about a thing will *determine* how it looks to one. It is not the case that if one sees that the object in front of one is a tree it follows that it looks to one like a tree; it may or may not do so.

I began this discussion of the place of inference, if any, in perception because I said that in learning to see something in a certain way the seeing was *grounded* on experience, and I wanted to make clear that I did not mean thereby that the seeing-as in question was the result of an inference from that experience. It is necessary, however, that I do say what I mean by it, and in a way that distinguishes the way of seeing's being grounded on experience from its being merely caused by it. For if the way of seeing is simply caused by an experience in the sense that one might say it is triggered by it, there are no grounds for saying that learning has really taken place. The triggering would be akin to what Plato seems mainly to have in mind when he spoke of our coming to know things by being reminded of them, according to his theory of recollection. It would be odd in any case to suggest that learning is a matter of being reminded of something, because in that case nothing really new is being attained. But if the experience simply acts as a trigger for calling up an insight, whether or not new, and there is no necessary connection between the content of the experience and the insight, it is still odd to suggest that learning has taken place. That consideration suggests that what is important for learning is that there should, at the very least, be a connection of content between the insight and the experience, and that it is this which makes it pertinent to say that the way of seeing that the insight consists in is grounded on the experience.

In this way the experience constitutes a reason for seeing whatever it is in that way. To speak of reasons here is not to exclude the possibility that causality has a place in the process. As is well known in connection with reasons for action, and has been emphasised by Donald Davidson in that context,[6] if a reason is to be efficacious, the having of it must have a causal role in the generation of the action in question. But the causality operates via a connection of content and not independently of that. Whether or not one wants to construe seeing something in a certain way as a form of doing something and thereby an action, the reference to reasons for action may be illuminating in the present context, in that it does not seem right to hold that when one does something for a reason one necessarily infers that this is the thing to do from the consideration adduced as the reason. One may do it because in the circumstances this is the thing to do, and philosophers often invoke in that connection the idea of the practical syllogism which Aristotle set out in his account of practical reason (and its occasional break-down in *akrasia* or weakness of will). It would be quite wrong, however, to suggest that in all action for a reason the person involved goes through a full-blown process of setting out principles and descriptions of the particular circumstances in such a way as to use them as premisses for an inference to a conclusion about what he or she should do. The practical syllogism is better construed as a reconstruction of the principles of the action, not as an account of what actually takes place. Hence too the reason that the person has for doing whatever he or she does does not function as a premiss for an inference about what is to be done.

If one can have a reason for seeing something in a new way without this involving an inference, there is nothing against the suggestion that an experience can function in a similar way in the acquisition of a new way of seeing in perceptual learning, and that as a result the new way of seeing is grounded on the experience. There is indeed nothing against the suggestion in connection with learning in general, in spite of Jerry Fodor's claim in the context of learning new concepts that the only way that this can be done is by some form of inference, particularly abduction or inference to the best explanation.[7] All that must be ruled out is the triggering which I mentioned earlier, in which the experience acts as a cause without there being any connection of content. St Paul's vision on the road to Damascus would indeed be a miracle, and so quite inexplicable without appeal to such a notion, if there was nothing in his experience which had a connection of content with his subsequent beliefs. There must have been something there, one might say, which made him see things in a different way from that point onwards. But when one says that, one is normally looking for something about the experience that explains the subsequent way of seeing things in a way that makes the connection between the two things intelligible.

It may be useful here to consider what may happen in cases of problem solving, like finding the answer to crossword clues. For in that case one is normally being required to see a connection between what is set out cryptically in the clue and the intended solution. Very often one is required to look at the clue and come to understand it in a way that is not the obvious one; then the solution comes via a new way of seeing things. (It is also of some interest, in connection with what cognitive scientists have come to describe as sub-doxastic processes, that often the solution and the new way of seeing come without our knowing exactly why. It is as if the brain goes on functioning without reference to any conscious processes. Nevertheless, the brain's processing (a processing of information in one sense of that term) is determined by a problem which was set for consciousness in the first place, and it is only because of this that one can speak of sub-doxastic processes on the analogy of full-blown doxastic processes in which one operates consciously on information in the ordinary sense of that word.) It is not at all extravagant to say that in arriving at the solution to the clue (and the situation may be similar in other cases of problem solving) learning is taking place, without this involving any obvious process of inference. Rather, something that we happen to see about the clue suggests to us a new way of construing it and, as a result, a new insight. That way of putting it is fine as long as this is a real process of suggestion, which is explicable in terms of its content, and not a mere triggering.

But that connection of content must not be such that it is as if one says to oneself 'It is like this, so it must also be like that.' There is no actual process of inference involved. In the case of crossword solving, for example, one can sometimes come to see what the solution is without knowing why; or alternatively one can come to see that the clue is to be construed in a certain way, again without knowing why. That rules out any possibility of inference being involved, even unconscious inference. But for the seeing to be a genuine case, the insight must have something to do with the way in which one has previously seen whatever is in question; there must be a connection of content. Familiarity, it is said, breeds contempt; it can also make a way of perceiving things seem satisfactory or acceptable, when it was not so before. But in many crucial cases, the acceptability is a product of perceiving something as an instance of a principle of organisation, which one did not see as applicable before, whether or not the perception is explicit and formulable. Thus, to give an example from my own experience, for one whose appreciation of music is embedded in tonal principles (something which, I believe is itself a product of learning) atonal music, particularly serial music, may sound wrong. But it can come to sound all right, and not just because an increased exposure to it may produce familiarity. In the case of serial music one can sometimes come to be able to hear the tone row, or at any rate come to appreciate that there is a reason why the notes are organised as they are, and thereby hear the music accordingly. Then a dissonance will not seem to want resolution. This, if it happens, is neither just familiarity nor magic; learning in a genuine sense has gone on.

That is to say, in the case in question, that one has come to hear the notes, not as organised on tonal principles, but in some different way. Because a musical note is not separable from the other notes which give it a context, one has come in this case to hear it as part of a new system of organisation. One hears the note in question as, in that sense, something new, as demanding new relationships, and so hears it as belonging where one would not have heard it before. That 'so' indicates that one hears it in the latter way *because* one hears it in the former way. But that 'because' should not be taken as suggesting that the connection is simply causal; nor is it a matter of inference. There is, so to speak, a rational principle involved, which makes the connection more than causal, but the rational principle does not function as a premiss in an inference or argument.

The case which I have discussed here is one (or so I believe) in which one way in which one has learnt to perceive things is supplanted, as the result of further learning, by a new way of perceiving them. There are also cases in which there is a natural, non-learned, way of seeing things which can be overriden by learning. In the case of the Müller-Lyer illusion, in which it is natural to see the lines with opposing arrow-heads on them as of different length (arguably because of purely sensory processes), one can learn to see them as of the same length. Here it is important to note that I speak of seeing them *as* of the same length, not of seeing *that* they are of the same length. The latter might come about because one says to oneself 'Oh, they look of different length because the arrow heads pull one's attention in different directions; if one disregards that, it must become apparent that they are really of the same length'. I do not say that it is always like that, but it is one definite possibility. One *sees* that the lines are of the same length because one is attending to perceptual considerations; one might know that the lines are of the same length because of reliable testimony to that effect, without *seeing* that they are. But one can see that they are of the same length without being able to see them in that way (and it is interesting that it is feasible to speak of *being able* so to see them). To see the lines *as* of the same length one has to bring the concept 'of same length' into active relation with the perceptual experience, so that it, so to speak, enforms it. One might do that as the result of the application of a technique, such as is involved in disregarding the arrow-heads. That means that there is involved an aspect of skill, which is of itself enough to justify speaking of learning here. Nevertheless, the skill involved is a perceptual skill. One learns to see the lines as if they had no arrow-heads on them, and it is because one sees the lines in that way that one can see them as of equal length.

That does not follow automatically, as one might expect it to do if that 'because' indicated a merely causal connection. Indeed, it is possible for someone to apply the skill in question and thus come to be able to see the lines as if without the arrow-heads attached to them, and still not be able to see them as of equal length. This, however, would then be for some different reasons from the simple overriding of the facts of sensory organisation which were (arguably) responsible for the illusion in the first place. That is to say that it would not be a matter of 'The illusion occurs because of the way in which the purely sensory experience is determined; the perceiver has learnt to override that, because selective attention enables him or her to limit the effects of that purely sensory experience on the total (conceptually organised) perceptual experience'. That is the way in which it works when someone has learnt to see the lines as of the same length. Hence, where that particular experience does not result it is likely to be due to some defect either in the person's vision (the workings of his or her visual apparatus) or because of an inability, however explained, to apply the relevant concept to the lines (perhaps the person just does not have the concept of 'equal length'). That would not, however, be the normal case. Normally, if the facts about the lines are what they are, and there is no question of conceptual defect, then if one has learnt to see the lines in one way (so that the arrow-heads are not intrinsic to them) one thereby comes, and so has learnt, to see them in another (as of equal length).

The example perhaps indicates, as clearly as any would, that learning to see things as such and suches may involve a number of different things. It may be a matter simply of coming to be able to apply a new concept to what is perceived, so that the total perceptual experience (as conceptually organised) changes too in a way that is appropriate to the object in question. In that sense there has been acquired a new way of understanding which is embodied in the perception. Perhaps my earlier example of learning to hear music as serial rather than tonal is of that kind. But in the example of learning to see the Müller-Lyer illusion lines as of equal length it is not obviously a matter of applying new concepts or principles of understanding. The concept applied is of course not one that is naturally applied, given the way in which one's experience is naturally structured. What one learns in this case is to apply a technique, involving attention, in such a way that some elements of what it is natural in this way to perceive are disregarded. This in turn makes the application of the concept 'equal length' the one appropriate to apply, and not the one which is natural in terms of sensory organisation. But it is because the technique involves learning (it involves an acquired skill involving the use of attention) that the resulting perception can be said to be the product of learning. Thus learning can figure in perception in as many ways as there are elements in that perception which can be a focus for learning.

To the extent that learning involves a new *use* of concepts, attention, and/or the organisation of experience, it is active and this implies that there must be an active aspect, as noted earlier, to perception itself. This can be accepted, whether or not learning is always itself an active business. We need not here adjudicate on whether circumstances might simply bring about changes in an individual such that it is appropriate to say that he or she has thereby learnt something. Personally, I am inclined to the view that there must always be something active involved. But as far as perception is concerned, my discussion ought to have indicated that in perceptual learning there is at any rate often some active process involved. This justifies my turning to my next topic – the part played by agency in perception.

Notes

1 The latter aspects of perception were a cardinal feature of the so-called 'new look' approach to perception which was adopted by some psychologists, including Jerome Bruner, in the '40s and '50s. It was claimed, for example, that something might be seen as bigger than it might otherwise have looked if it was also seen as particularly valuable. See e.g. Bruner, Jerome S. (1974), *Beyond the Information Given*, Allen and Unwin: London, chapter 2.

2 See some of the papers in Part II of my (1983), *Perception, Learning and the Self,* Routledge and Kegan Paul: London.

3 In a recent book by Robert Schwartz ((1994), *Vision*, Blackwell: Oxford, p.93), it is said, in discussing the views of Helmholtz, that for him 'The assumption was – and for many theorists still is – that learning cannot affect our senses per se.' It is also suggested that J.J. Gibson has shown that things are otherwise. Whether or not that is a correct assessment of Gibson, who, after all, thought of the senses as perceptual systems the function of which is both to seek and derive information from the environment, the statement may be confusing to many. Much depends on what a sense is, but, however much learning affects perception, does it affect sense-organs or their working?

4 On this see further my 'Unconscious inference and judgment in perception', included in my (1983), *Perception, Learning and the Self*, Routledge and Kegan Paul: London, pp.11–29.

5 I say 'ought to be' because the principle mentioned was stated in connection with space perception and he was led to say that spatial attributes are not 'sensational' but the result of 'habit and experience'. Colour attributes remained 'sensational' for him, although it is less than clear how they could be, given his account of colour contrast.

6 Davidson, D., 'Actions, reasons and causes', in his (1980), *Essays on Actions and Events*, Clarendon Press: Oxford, pp.3–19. The way in which I have put the matter is not quite Davidson's or that of a whole host of philosophers who have followed him over this issue, since it has been taken by them as showing that reasons are themselves causes, rather than that the having of a reason may be this.

7 See Fodor, J. (1983), *Representations*, Bradford Books, MIT Press: Cambridge, Mass. and (1987), *Psychosemantics*, Bradford Books, MIT Press Cambridge, Mass.

Chapter 9
The role of agency

There are various ways in which activity on our part in some form may seem to play an essential role in enabling us to gain adequate perception of the world. I have already referred, for example, to the role played by attention, when we actively turn our attention to one thing or one aspect of what we are perceiving rather than another. More obvious still, perhaps, is the fact that we can and do turn our eyes or head in the direction of what is to be perceived; we move our hands or other limbs in order to get better tactual perception of what we feel; and we may move our tongues over something in our mouth in order to taste it better. All these are ways in which activity on our part enables us to perceive the world better or at least differently. To say this is not quite to say that the activity is essential if perception is to take place at all.

Some psychologists have stressed the role of action or activity in perception. Jean Piaget, for example, produced a theory according to which the intellect, as he put it, has to play an active role in correcting what may otherwise be the distorting, as well as enabling, role of the sensory mechanisms. Jerome Bruner has emphasised the part played by activity in going 'beyond the information given', while James Gibson, at any rate in his second book *The Senses Considered as Perceptual Systems* spoke of the role of perceptual systems in hunting for stimuli.[1] The general assumption on the part of these thinkers is that an account of what is simply presented to the senses is not enough to explain our ability to perceive the world as we do. I have myself indicated in the foregoing various things, including the possession and use of concepts, which is also required, but more argument is perhaps required if it is to be taken as shown that in perception we are not just passive beings. Are the considerations that these psychologists have adduced more than ones which show how we are enabled to perceive the world *better*? There is no point in trying to arrive at an adjudication on that issue here. It is important, however, that the distinction between what enables us to perceive better and what enables us to perceive at all should be appreciated.[2]

It can be taken for granted that action on our part enables us to perceive the world better. It is indeed clear that our bodily reactions are, as it were, tuned to our normal ways of perceiving things, to the extent that it is sometimes very difficult to override those reactions when what we perceive is not quite as we normally perceive it. That is most obvious, perhaps, in the familiar phenomenon of not being able to step properly on to a stationary escalator. Our normal bodily reactions to the perception of the bottom or top of an escalator, our bodily readiness to counteract the moving surface on which we step, still take place even though we clearly see the escalator as stationary. It would be wrong, therefore, to produce a supposed account of perception, which did not situate perception in a context which takes into account the body and bodily reactions.3 It would be equally wrong, however, to attempt to construe perception entirely in terms of possible bodily reactions. To perceive something is not to be disposed to react to it in certain ways, even if a perception of many things does bring into play bodily reactions and could not be understood properly except in such a context.

The question at issue is whether a purely passive being could perceive the world, or, put the matter in a rather different way, whether an account of perception which paid attention only to processes which are plausibly considered as merely passive would be adequate as an account of perception of the *world*. I put the matter in this latter way because some recent accounts of perception which seek to understand it in terms of information processing and see such processes as computational might be thought of as appealing to processes which are simply passive.4 Let us suppose that a theory can be produced which adequately explains in computational terms how such things as the edges of objects can be distinguished. This would be a theory concerned with perception of the spatial aspects of things in so far as that spatial conception confines itself to what might be called geometrical or perhaps topological considerations. It would explain how it is possible for us to distinguish in certain respects one part of the field of vision from another. Because we have two eyes separated from each other there occurs retinal disparity, and this, along with other things, goes part of the way towards explaining the possibility of distance perception. It goes part of the way only, however, because without concepts of depth and distance the perceiver could make no sense of the cues provided.

Berkeley, as is well known, thought that sight by itself could provide no idea of distance, for a variety of reasons, but particularly because the projection of objects perceived on to the retina is on to a two-dimensional surface only.5 He maintained that the perception of distance is mediated only by touch, and in particular through tactual perception made possible through movement. The terms of reference for Berkeley's theory, involving considerations of where we get our ideas from, are themselves suspect, but in any case later thinkers have tried to indicate that there are features of our vision which make perception of distance possible by other means. By these I do not means the sort of so-called cues, such as retinal disparity which I have already mentioned. Berkeley already knew much about these and argued that there was nothing in such considerations which indicated that they could be by themselves a source of ideas of distance; it would be another matter once

64

given such ideas derived from some other source.

Gibson, in his first book, *The Perception of the Visual World*,6 pointed to certain features of what are in effect visual phenomenology, which he thought were enough in themselves to show how our perception of distance can arise. As long as we take account of the ground on which objects at various distances lie, and do not confine ourselves, as he thought classical optics did, to objects seen, as it were, in the air without reference to their background, we can see that objects at varying distances form a sort of gradient as far as concerns their perceived size. But of course, unless we knew something about those objects and their actual size, unless we knew, for example, that there is no necessary connection between the distance of an object and its actual size (whatever be the connection between its distance and its perceived or apparent size), such considerations would not be enough to give us any idea of their distance. Indeed, unless we know something about objects as such, including the fact that they occupy space, nothing about their apparent relative sizes could give us any idea of the fact that there is such a thing as distance. So nothing about visual phenomenology, unless it is presupposed that it involves space-occupying objects, could be sufficient to make possible distance perception. But if we have the conception of space-occupying objects, we must already have some idea of distance, since those objects are three-dimensional.

I suggested earlier that Berkeley's question about the source of our ideas of distance is misconceived. One might well ask what there is about touch, even active touch, which could provide us with the idea of distance, if we did not know already that in moving our hands, say, over objects and in moving our bodies in general we were indeed moving through space. Kant, following in this respect rationalist philosophers, maintained that our concept of space was *apriori*. He did not mean by this that our idea of space is necessarily innate, and he was careful to say at the beginning of the Introduction to the second edition of his *Critique of Pure Reason* (B1) that 'Though all our knowledge begins with experience, it does not follow that it all arises out of experience'. To say that an idea is *apriori* is in itself simply to make the negative claim that its source is not experience. Nevertheless, that still presupposes that it makes sense to ask what are the sources of an idea; it presupposes that there is something from which it can be thought to be derived. There is of course always a question of how a thought is to be given flesh, so to speak, how it is related to whatever constitutes its exemplification or application, and how, if at all, it is manifested in experience. Moreover, once given certain thoughts, it is reasonable to suppose that experience will enable us to have others which are relevant to it. But that is not to say that there is any question of there being a single source for any idea, even if experience is more obviously and closely relevant to some ideas than it is to others.

We should not ask, therefore, what there is in experience which is sufficient to enable us to perceive things as at a distance from us. We can nevertheless ask what sense a perceiver could make of a world of objects at distance if he or she could not move around that world or at least move in such a way as to manipulate those objects. That brings me back to my question whether the idea of a purely passive perceiver makes sense, and *a fortiori* whether it is enough to construe perception entirely in terms of what affects the senses, even if subsequent processes, perhaps of so-called information retrieval, modify that. It is clear enough that features of our sense-organs, such as the fact that the retina of the eye forms a two-dimensional manifold, that we have two eyes, two ears and so on, structure our perception of the world in certain ways. The question how this enables us to perceive things at a distance simply presents in a particular crucial way the problem of the relation of these structural facts to our perception of a world which is also structured, but not in quite the same way. Even if we allow that vision presents us with a two-dimensional array there is still a question of the relation of the features of that array to our perception of things as to the left, right, up and down, and so on. After all, to say that an object is towards the left is to place it in relation to one's body, but to say that something is towards the left of one's field of vision may be to place it more towards the right of one's body if one's eyes are turned to the right, even if it is to the left of other objects in one's field of vision.[7]

The lay-out of objects in one's field of vision should correspond to the lay-out of the pattern of stimulation on the retinae of one's eyes, but for the inverting function of the lens of the eye, if the circumstances of the visual perception are normal, and not distorted by any external device such as distorting spectacles. That is simply a fact of optics. It is not similarly a fact of optics that we are able to see a world of objects standing in spatial relationships, as well as having other properties. What we thus see is not simply a patterned array. The Gestalt Psychologists emphasised that we tend to see what we see in terms of organised patterns, constituting 'wholes' or *Gestalten*. They also drew attention to the fact that we tend to see figures against a ground or background, and that the difference between the two is a function of the organisation of the material. I once argued that this was an analytic consequence of what is involved in the idea of perceiving an object.[8] But seeing one object (a real object) as lying behind another is quite a different matter from seeing a figure against a ground.[9] The figure-ground relationship is simply a function of the organisation of the perceptual array, while seeing one object as lying behind another is not merely that. Seeing objects as standing in spatial relationships presupposes an understanding of the nature of objects as well as the nature of spatial relationships. Indeed, one might say that these two things must come together.

As already noted, objects do not normally change their size simply by being moved about; in particular they do not normally change their size in being located further from or nearer to us. This fact that objects do not normally change size when undergoing simple spatial transitions is one of the facts that Piaget appealed to in his conservation studies, as something that the child has to come to appreciate during his or her intellectual development.[10] What the child in fact has to learn in this respect is something about the criteria of identity for physical objects – that spatial location by itself is irrelevant to the transformations that an identical object can undergo. That of course is not to say that changes of spatial location may not affect how an object looks, though there is no simple relationship between, for example, apparent size and distance. But without some appreciation of what is involved in the identity of physical objects there can be no real appreciation of what it is for such objects to stand in spatial relations. The perception of a spatial world is not the perception of simply formal or geometrical relations; it is the perception of a *world* which not only has a spatial lay-out but is occupied by physical objects.

What has this to do with agency? Berkeley, it will be remembered, insisted on the part played by movement in the acquisition of the idea of distance, and I have already indicated that movement by itself would not do the trick unless there were some appreciation already on the part of the perceiver that he or she was making the movements through space. Since, however, that space is not simply a system of formal relationships, but something that is occupied by physical bodies, the relationship between oneself and those physical bodies must come into the picture. Such a relationship is not to be construed as a purely causal one, although the relationship which I have in mind would not be possible unless there were also causal connections between our body and other bodies. To understand something as a physical body is of course to understand what it is for such a thing to affect and be affected by other things, but for present purposes what is more important in this respect is an understanding of what it is for us to operate with other bodies and for them to frustrate or facilitate such operations. And that is manifestly a function of agency on our part. To perceive a physical object is not simply to perceive something as resistant to the will; for many of the things that we perceive as physical objects the question of whether they do or would resist the will simply does not arise for us. The idea of a physical object is not just the idea of something that can or does resist the will, as is implicit in the suggestion, mentioned earlier as made by Maine de Biran, that the idea of physical objects comes only in relation to their role in relation to an *effort voulu*. To say this, however, does not go against the point that we should have no idea of physical objects if we had not learnt what it is for things to be manipulable or non-manipulable via an interaction between them and our bodies.

That could not be all there was to a conception of them as spatial. For that, it would at least have to be the case that the manipulation in question was itself spatial and somehow conceived as such. It is not my concern here to speculate about how such a conception could arise, but it is fairly clear that movements of the kind which we make in such manipulation go together with the effects which they have on the objects in question and the effects that these have on us. It is a genuine interaction which is involved, and the mere making of movements which are in fact spatial (as are the limb-movements of a newborn child) would not be enough for a conception of space to arise. For there would be nothing to mark what is involved in space-occupancy. (A child could of course use one part of its body in interaction with another part and this might be genuine interaction; the body interacted with does not have to be *another* body. But that does not affect the general principle that an appreciation of space-occupancy requires bodily interaction of an active kind.) Once given a general understanding of a world of physical objects occupying space it is no longer necessary that every object should always be seen in terms of the relations of this kind that it has with us and our bodies. My point is rather that unless *some* objects were seen this way there could be no general conception of a physical world involving spatial relations with objects occupying space. It is in this way that the essential role of agency comes into the picture.

On the other hand, it is not just spatial perception which turns on such considerations. The perception of colour, for example, in so far as it is not just the perception of coloured light, depends on the way in which colour is related to the objects so coloured. Solid objects, which is what to some extent or another physical objects are, are seen as coloured by way of a perception of such colours extending over at least part of the surface of such objects. That is why this kind of colour has been called 'surface colour' by contrast with 'film colours', the colour of liquids, gases or transparent objects, where the colour is seen as permeating or extending through the object in question. Even in the latter case, however, the colour is seen as having a relation to a spatial feature of the object. Colours are thus see as extending over the surfaces of objects or extending through them when it is possible to see through them. Thus the perception of colour is not independent of the perception of the physically manifested spatial features of objects. In the case of other senses, the situation may be different in detail but not in general. Sounds are emitted from objects and can be heard as such, but they can be heard in relative independence from the objects which produce or reflect them. But they are normally heard as from a direction even if that is diffuse, and it is questionable whether it would be right to speak of an auditory perception of *sound* at all if there were no conception on the part of the hearer of he production of sounds. Similar things apply to smell.

(This issue has been mixed up with the question whether the senses can be said to have proper objects (Berkeley) or special objects (Aristotle, for which see chapter 6), a question which tends to have other implications and presuppositions. The way in which sound is related to hearing is not quite the same as the way in which colour is related to sight, if only because sounds can be heard in relative independence of the objects which produce them. Smells, even more so, can persist when what produces them has gone. These factors are a function of the physical processes which are involved causally in the form of perception in question. It remains true that one can hear a sound or smell a smell without any awareness of what produces them. That is true of the visual perception of colour only to a limited extent, as when a coloured light fills our field of vision; mostly it is otherwise. Philosophers concerned with proper or special objects of the senses have had trouble in this connection with the objects of touch, having recourse to such things as 'tangible qualities'; but these are obviously not independent of the bodies which have them.)

Even when one perceives something in relative independence from the physical things which produce them or to which they are otherwise causally related, that independence remains relative only. It is not an absolute independence, and the phenomenon does not provide a counter-example to the thesis that perception would

68

not be possible in general unless there were an interaction between our bodies and the bodies of which the world is made up. Since that interaction, as I have insisted, is an active one, it is not a counter-example either to the thesis that perception presupposes agency on the part of the perceiver. Let me emphasise again, however, what this does *not* mean. It is not that every case of perception involves activity, nor even that most or many such cases involve that. It is simply that a perceiver must be an agent, and that the attempt to account for perception by reference throughout to processes which are passive in nature will not do. Moreover, this is quite separate from the question whether activity on our part may not in many cases enable us to perceive things, or at any rate some things, better than we might otherwise have done.

Notes

1 Piaget, Jean, (1969), *The Mechanisms of Perception*, Routledge and Kegan Paul: London; Bruner, Jerome (1974), *Beyond the Information Given*, Anglin, J.M. (ed.), Allen and Unwin: London;Gibson, J.J. (1966), *The Senses Considered as Perceptual Systems*, Houghton Mifflin: Boston. It should perhaps be noted that in this last mentioned book Gibson's philosophical leanings were by and large realist; the world is there waiting to be perceived, so to speak. There were in it, however, already suggestions of the use of a concept, that of 'affordances', which became the centre piece of his last book, (1979), *The Ecological Approach to Visual Perception*, Houghton Mifflin: Boston. According to that book an account of perception is itself part of an account of our ecology, the way in which we are enabled to make our way in the environment. Things, construed as affordances are simply things in so far as they afford that possibility. The ground is, for example, simply that which affords us support. Strictly speaking, on this theory of perception, we do not perceive things realistically construed, but only things in so far as they make perception and behaviour in relation to them possible. This in effect presupposes a pragmatist and not realist view of perception and the world.

2 On this and related matters see my 'Perception and agency' and other papers in Part I of my (1983), *Perception, Learning and the Self*, Routledge and Kegan Paul: London; also my (1990), *In and Out of the Black Box*, Basil Blackwell: Oxford, pp.99–107.

3 Among philosophers it is perhaps Maurice Merleau-Ponty who has put most stress on the role of the body in perception. See his (1962), *The Phenomenology of Perception*, trans. Colin Smith, Routledge and Kegan Paul: London. An earlier French philosopher who, for somewhat different reasons, emphasised the part played by bodily action in our perception of the world is Maine de Biran; he thought that our perception of physical objects was a function of an *effort voulu*.

4 The most well known example of such an account is that produced by the late

David Marr in his (1982), *Vision*, W.H. Freeman: San Francisco. What I go on to discuss is a theory *like* his, without necessarily implying that he would have accepted everything that I say in my account of such a theory. See my *In and Out of the Black Box*, pp.75ff.

5 There is a good discussion of Berkeley's theory in Schwartz, Robert (1994), *Vision*, Blackwell: Oxford.

6 Gibson, J.J. (1950), *The Perception of the Visual World*, Houghton Mifflin: Boston.

7 In his first book Gibson made a distinction between the visual world and the visual field. I have spoken of one's field of vision and not one's visual field. I have doubts about the whole notion of the visual field, which Gibson says is something we can be aware of when we see things in perspective or as the painter sees them; it is as if what is there consists of 'areas of colored surface, divided up by contours' and is supposed to correspond the the pattern of retinal stimulation. See my (1957), 'The visual field and perception', *Proc. Arist. Soc,*. Supp. Vol. 31, pp.107–24.

8 See my (1957), *The Psychology of Perception*, Routledge and Kegan Paul: London, pp.55ff. Richard Wollheim has offered some criticism of that suggestion, pointing to the particular phenomenon of seeing a drawing or painting as lying on or in front of the canvas on which it is drawn or painted. See e.g. his (1973), 'On drawing an object' in *On Art and the Mind*, Allen Lane: London, pp.3–30.

9 It is arguable, however, that one could not see a figure, *qua* representation, against a ground unless one had some idea of what it is for an object to lie behind another.

10 For a discussion of these see my (1978), *Experience and the Growth of Understanding*, Routledge and Kegan Paul: London, chapter 4.

Chapter 10
Consciousness and attention

In much of what I have so far said the role of consciousness has been at least implicit. I spoke earlier about intentionality – the fact that perception is or can be 'of' things, whether or not those things exist *in rerum natura* as physical objects. But intentionality in this sense is not in itself consciousness. In the first place it has long been recognised that there is such a thing as unconscious or subliminal perception. Leibniz, for example, argued in support of the idea of unconscious perception and of what he called '*petites perceptions*' (forms of perception which are part of a complex perceptual process and which are not distinguished as such, as in the case, to use his own example, of perception of the noise made by the waves of the sea, in which the sound produced by each wave is not distinguished although it is in some way heard). In some cases of the latter phenomenon one may, in retrospect, come to realise that one has actually heard a constituent sound without being explicitly aware of it at the time; that can be the case in hearing music, particularly orchestral music. The same can be true of the visual perception of a complex scene. Subliminal perception can, likewise, occur when what is perceived does not immediately register. This can be for a variety of reasons; for example, the illumination or sound level may be too low, the object in question may appear only momentarily, what is perceived may be too complex to take in all at once, or our attention may be focussed on other things. In all such cases there may be reason, either in what can be seen of the person's behaviour or in what he or she can be got to report in retrospect, for maintaining that the person does or did perceive whatever is in question without being immediately aware of doing so.

There is no real problem about this. The phenomena which I have so far mentioned are all ones in which something that is unconscious is part of or connected with a process of perception which is in general conscious. I have already noted ways in which one can explain the deviation from the pattern of conscious perception. It would be different if the unconscious perceptions were intrinsically unconscious and not related to anything conscious. I shall return to that point a

71

little later, but for the time being it may be worth while to give further consideration to the particular role of attention – to give more attention to that! Psychologists such as A.M. Treisman[1] have been concerned with the ways in which selective attention can figure in perceptual phenomena, so that one thing is explicitly perceived rather than another, or one way of perceiving something rather than another occupies one's attention (as is the case, probably, in at least some cases of ambiguous figures). It is natural in such cases to speak of our *directing* our attention to one thing rather than another, or perhaps, in some instances, of our attention *being directed* to one thing rather than another (when something, for example, attracts our attention in this way). Such direction of attention can be intentional, even deliberate, but it need not be so. In the cases in which our attention is attracted, drawn or even forced on us, so to speak, by something in our environment (including the activity of other people), the way in which our attention is directed is involuntary, though not something totally non-voluntary. Indeed, the attraction in question may in some cases be resisted. In the case of the perception of ambiguous figures, such as the well-known 'duck-rabbit' figure devised by Jastrow, seeing the figure in one way, e.g. as of a duck, may seem irresistible at first, but it is quite possible to learn to see it in the other way, as I indicated in an earlier discussion of the phenomenon, by the acquisition of some technique to that end; one may concentrate on some element in the figure which 'makes' it look one way rather than the other. (I put 'makes' in quotation marks to indicate that this is merely a useful device; there is no compulsion or necessity about it.)

The direction of attention may be associated with some bodily attitude as well – with, for example, a turning of the eyes in a certain direction. But, again, there is no necessity about that. In viewing some scene one may keep the eyes steady while paying attention to one part of the field of view rather than another, even a part which lies on the fringe of that field of view, and even when it is natural to have regard to what is at the centre. This is perhaps easier when one has some knowledge of what lies within the field of view, or at any rate when one is able to identify or characterise what is there, whether rightly or wrongly. That is in effect to say that the selective direction of attention is made easier by, whether or not it depends on, the application of concepts to what is there. This is because one naturally attends to things as such and suches, and attention is more easily held on to something when there is some description under which the thing is attended to. To say this is to indicate the extent to which attention, as a form of consciousness, involves intentionality. It is directed *to* something, and to capture it, so to speak, it is normally required that that thing should be brought under a concept or concepts, whether or not rightly.

In perception, whether or not one is attending selectively to what is there to be seen, consciousness is normally involved in some way, and if one is led to say that the perceiver (who may be oneself) perceives something that is there unconsciously this is against the background of the fact that perception is a form of consciousness. I do not mean by this that it involves self-consciousness; the extent

72

to which that is so, if at all, I shall return to in the next chapter. I do not mean, therefore, that in perceiving one has to be conscious of the fact that one is perceiving or even that one normally is so. The point is, rather, that perception involves in some way consciousness of its objects and of the way in which they are thereby regarded. To say that there is unconscious perception of an object to some effect is to say that there are grounds for attributing to the person concerned knowledge or belief, derived from that perception, about what falls within the field of perception, even though the person in question is not aware of having such knowledge or belief. It is of course true in that case that the person in question is not aware of the fact that he or she is perceiving whatever it is; but it is the fact that he or she is *perceiving that thing* which he or she is unaware of. It is not a matter of being unaware of perceiving at all.

But that brings me back to the point which I shelved when I began speaking of unconscious perception, the point about whether unconscious perception is possible which does not have a form of conscious perception as its background. It might be argued (and I have myself argued2) that an account of perception which makes it merely a matter of beliefs being brought about by stimulation of sense-organs is inadequate because it leaves out the experiential aspect of perception which is itself a function of perception being a form of consciousness. But this raises questions about what has come to be called 'blind sight' as a result of investigations originally carried out by Larry Weiskrantz.3 Some patients who have partial hemianopia because of brain damage are able to detect points of light which fall within the 'blind' section of the retina much more reliably than would be expected if it was just chance. The patients in question had no conception of being able to see the points of light and thought that they were guessing about them. (It is of course not without importance that the detection of the lights was nothing like 100 per cent reliable.) One possible explanation of the phenomenon that has been suggested is that there is some scattering of light within the eye so that the 'non-blind' part of the retina is somehow affected, but that of course does not gainsay the point that the patients in question had no awareness of any perceptual experience. Whatever the explanation of the phenomenon itself, the philosophical and conceptual point at issue is whether it constitutes a form of sight.

If the hypothesis is correct that the 'non-blind' part of the retina is affected by the lights in some way, this serves to explain how there can be visual functioning in spite of the fact that the 'blind' part of the retina, its connections with the brain and the relevant part of the brain itself are together non-functional. It might then be said that the stimulation of the functional part of the retina in the way suggested (which is, after all, not the normal way in which the retina is stimulated in order to produce sight) simply brings about a form of subliminal perception, and, moreover, one which is only partially reliable. The stimulation of the functional part of the retina is not at a sufficiently high level to register, so to speak, in consciousness. This would be unproblematic, in that the subliminal perception would occur in a context in which ordinary conscious perception is the norm; it would thus fit in with the conditions for subliminal perception that I specified earlier. *A fortiori* it would be quite wrong to make a meal of any notion of 'blind sight' in this case; the sight would not be blind but merely subliminal, and this would be quite consistent with the fact that the patients in question thought that they were merely guessing.

Let us suppose, however, that the hypothesis in question is not correct, nor is anything like it. Let us suppose instead that the light does affect the 'blind' part of the retina (which is, after all, blind only because of something in the brain, not because it is itself non-functional). We might also suppose that there are also functional connections with the brain, but not in the normal way, so that no conscious experience results. It may seem that it cannot be quite right to say that the patients are simply caused by the physical/physiological processes involved to have a belief that there are lights within what would normally be their field of vision, because they think that they are merely guessing. Of course there would be a question for them of whether or not there are lights in front of them, because the conditions of the test involve them having to give answers on that score. Thus it might be that they come to have beliefs but with no real degree of confidence about that. Nevertheless, it would be at least odd to suppose that they have such beliefs when the degree of confidence is nil. The notion of unconscious belief is not itself problematical, though many cases of unconscious belief involve beliefs which have been *put out of* consciousness (as is arguably the case with the Freudian concept of repression). If the patients have no reason, good or bad, for not wanting to recognise that they have the beliefs in question, what reason could *we* have for wanting to say that they must have those beliefs though unconsciously. The answer must lie in their behaviour; they do report lights correctly more frequently than would be expected if it was merely chance. Is that enough?

The answer to that question is problematic, though it may seem clear that *something* makes the patients give the responses that they do. As we have already seen, it often happens even to the normal-sighted that they may realise after the event that they have seen something without being conscious of doing so at the time. Sometimes indeed they may react in some way to something in their environment without being conscious of the reasons for so doing and without having any beliefs about that thing. It might be objected that I ought to say that they do so without having any beliefs that they are conscious of about that thing. But to insist on that would be to make behaviour too dependent on belief. The currently fashionable model for the explanation of behaviour is that such explanation comes via appeal to some combination of belief and desire. But even if it is granted that an appeal to a cognitive state by itself is not enough to explain behaviour without some reference to motivation as well, the paradigm in question is too rigid a one to take in all cases of behaviour. For example, it would be overdoing it to insist that in cases of mere habits the explanation of the behaviour comes via appeal to belief and desire. For that appeal to be pertinent the behaviour has to be at least intentional or at any rate involve an intentional action in some way (for it might be argued that unintentional action must involve a doing which is intentional under some description).

But an action which is performed out of habit is also likely to be such that it is because the circumstances are what they are that the habit is called out. Hence perception of what the circumstances are is part of the aetiology of the habit. Hence, although a habit is something in connection with which an appeal to beliefs may not be immediately relevant perceptual belief may come into the picture in explaining why the habit takes place in just these particular circumstances. What we need is something different – an account of a reaction to something in the environment where belief does not come into the picture at all, so that it is possible to meet the objection, mentioned above, that the belief is there although the person concerned is not conscious of having it. If the reaction is habitual it must be so without its being the case that it takes place because of a belief that the circumstances are thus and so. But in order for it to be true that the person concerned sees *that* the circumstances are thus and so must it not be the case that he or she believes that they are that? Moreover, how else could perception be involved at all?

The answer to the last question may be that not all reactions to the environment take place because the person concerned sees that something is the case. I may simply react to something in a certain way because I see it *as* such and such, without seeing *that* it is anything at all. Perhaps I have been trained so to do, and as a result of the training I react more or less mechanically, so to speak. But, of course, in the course of the training, and as part of it, I must have been got to react in the way in question when I saw that such and such was the case, even if as a result of the training I come so to react merely when I see whatever it is *as* whatever is relevant. If that is the case, we have here an example where belief-determined, and presumably conscious, perception is there in the background even if it is not apparent in the actual instance in question. How far is this relevant to cases of 'blind sight' if, on the hypothesis which I was considering, there are no grounds for thinking that appeal to the idea of subliminal perception is in place?

On the face of it, it is not relevant at all, because, even if it is admitted that the 'blind-sight' patients do have conscious perception when the functional parts of their retinae are stimulated, this conscious perception is quite disconnected, because of the brain damage, from the circumstances in which 'blind-sight' takes place. In the cases which I mentioned just now it is the training that connects the conscious, belief-determined perception with the subsequent reactions. There is, *ex hypothesi* no such connection or any relevant connection in the 'blind-sight' case. Hence unless there is some explanation for the reactions, along the lines of appeal to subliminal perception, as might be the case if the light affecting the 'blind' part of the retina is scattered in such a way as to affect the functional part, but only subliminally, it would seem out of place to speak of sight at all. Of course, the reactions of which I have spoken are not like reflex reactions or reactions to such things as pricks; they are not even straightforwardly bodily, they are reports about whether anything has been seen, though guesses as the patients suppose. But if the supposed guesses are too reliable really to be guesses, this would make the phenomena exceptionally puzzling, to a degree that makes recourse in some way to the idea of subliminal perception almost inevitable. But one thing seems fairly clear – where there is no question of at least subliminal perception, it seems wrong to speak of sight too.

What emerges from all this is that there is nothing wrong with the idea of unconscious perception provided that this is a deviation from the norm of conscious perception and the deviation can be explained in an intelligible way – by, for example, indicating that what there was to be seen was too faint or too mixed up with other things to be taken in in such a way as to be explicit. But if someone had no conscious perception at all, there would be no case for ever speaking of unconscious perception in his or her case. Moreover, if the supposed instances of unconscious perception manifested by a person, when there was stimulation of locally non-functional parts of the visual system, were radically disconnected from the rest of his or her conscious perception, as would be the case if the 'blind-sight' was not to be explained by reference to some form of subliminal perception, there would in fact be no case for speaking of perception at all, let alone unconscious perception, in their case. How one *should* speak of these cases is another matter; the 'blind-sight' in question would not be real sight, but something more like stimulation-produced clairvoyance! But unconscious perception can be invoked in given circumstances provided that the person in question has conscious perception in general, and provided that there is a genuine way of explaining the deviation from the norm.

With this in mind, let us return to the forms of selective consciousness which are typical of attention. Normally, as indicated earlier, when one is confronted with an array of objects within the field of view, one attends to some of them rather than others. To what extent one's attention is restricted in that way is an empirical matter. It is logically possible that someone might be able to attend equally to everything in his or her field of view, but it is very unlikely to be the case in fact. The attempt to spread one's attention is likely to have the effect that the level of attention is diminished or even minimalised. But much turns here on what one has in mind and on what one is expecting to see, as well as on one's general understanding of what is in one's environment. In the case of hearing, the question has been raised as to whether, and to what extent, it is possible to follow, attend to, more than one line of counterpoint in music. Is it the case that following more than one such line is a matter of shifting one's attention from one line to another in alternation? I see no reason why the latter must be the case. One *can* attend to more than one thing at the same time, but the extent to which that is possible is obviously conditioned by the complexity of the things in question, especially if we are concerned with how they are over time.

On the other hand, it is unlikely that one would be able to attend to two lines of counterpart at the same time unless one had some idea, some knowledge, of what one was attending to. It might be the case that, for a short time perhaps, the division of the music into two distinct lines was so obvious that the fact was forced upon us, so to speak. The likelihood of that effect might be increased if there were spatial separation between the sounds in question, as there often is in Gabrielli's music, for example. Even so, one must know what a line of music amounts to so that the notes are not heard merely as a jumble of sounds, whatever their origin. So the forcing of the phenomenon on us still depends on a general understanding of what is going on. It is of course the case that sometimes the intensity of a light or sound may bring it about that we attend to it without our having any real understanding of what it is, other than that it is a phenomenon of sight or sound. But once we begin to differentiate between different aspects of what is seen or heard, whether or not we attend to them differentially, the understanding is brought to bear, even if the concepts involved in that are rudimentary, so that we are aware of what is there simply as this rather than that.

It follows from all this that even if consciousness *can* play a role, in respect of our relations with the environment, such that there is, so to speak, merely the registration that there is something there, there are no grounds so far for speaking of perception, unless and until what is there is distinguished. It is also only when a differentiation of something in the environment takes place in that way that there can be in consequence some form of behavioural reaction which is perception-dependent. But whether or not there is an overt behavioural reaction, consciousness of something as a such and such depends on the possession of concepts relevant to something's being a such and such. If someone wants to insist that, when there is simply that registration of something which I mentioned just now, our attention, and therefore our consciousness, is so to speak grabbed by whatever it is without this requiring concepts, that point is not to be denied. It is not that all consciousness requires concepts; it is that the consciousness will not be perceptual consciousness unless and until that is the case. That is not just a boring point of verbal legislation; it is fundamental to an understanding of what perception involves.

The point is also relevant to an issue which I have discussed elsewhere,[4] but which I shall only mention here, though some of the material of chapter 8 is relevant to it. That is the issue how if perception involves concepts and if the acquisition of concepts depends on experience an understanding of the world and equally perception of it can come about at all. The regress or circle that seems implicit in the mutual dependence of experience and concepts can be met by the consideration that that mutual dependence is a logical or conceptual dependence and has no necessary implications of a temporal kind. It is not that we must first have concepts in order to have perception and first have perception in order to have concepts. As far as concerns the growth of experience and understanding the two may come together, temporally speaking, but neither will be present unless and until the other one is. Nevertheless, it seems clear that if perception is to develop there must be forms of attention to the environment from which perception proper emerges. I have spoken of cases in which our consciousness of something is attracted by t he fact that the light or sound involved is of an outstanding intensity. Something similar might be the case with infants in whom perception, and perhaps even the focussing of the eyes, have not yet developed.[5] How that develops into perception of what is there as a such and such is a difficult question, but no doubt that development presupposes the more basic phenomenon of attention being drawn to something without consciousness of that something *as* anything. One basic form of attention need not even involve consciousness of anything as an object, but merely consciousness of an experience (a sensation, one might say); for that reason it cannot be considered as a form of perception. That indeed is, in a way, a fundamental point about the relation between *perception* and consciousness – that whether or not perception is conscious, it presupposes the possibility of being conscious of an object as an object. More than that, if perception is really to be considered as taking place, the object must be taken as one of a particular kind, in which case concepts certainly come into play. This is without prejudice to the possibility of attention being drawn to something without consciousness of it *as* anything, whether or not that counts as perception and whether or not the development of perception presupposes such a thing.

There are thus three ways in which consciousness or attention may enter into phenomena having to do with perception. There is, first, the consciousness involved in having an experience or sensation, when there need be no question of being aware of it as this rather than that and thus equally no question of it being concept-dependent. (Which is not to deny that sometimes one *may* be aware of a sensation as one of a particular kind rather than another.) In this case there is no perceptual object and thus no intentionality; indeed, as I suggested in chapter 3, attention to sensations that one is having may make one insensitive to the properties of an object perception of which may be mediated by those sensations. Attention to the feelings in one's finger-tips may make one insensitive to the properties of the surface over which one is running one's fingers. It can equally work the other way; attention to the object in question may make one insensitive to the sensations which one is having in the process. That indeed is the norm in perception, and in the case of vision, for example, one is rarely if ever conscious of the sensation-like experiences that one is having. Hence, apart from the examples of pains or irritations that one may cease to be conscious of, as noted in chapter 3, when one's attention is elsewhere, there may be genuine cases of unconscious sensation.6

There is, second, consciousness of an object, but not as a such and such, so that the object figures in the consciousness only indeterminately. In this case too no concepts are involved except, it might be suggested, the completely general concept of an object. That, however, is no proper concept; it is at best a formal concept, to invoke the idea that Wittgenstein put forward in his *Tractatus* 4.126. Nevertheless, the consideration that underlies the suggestion is not an empty one; to have this form of consciousness there must be at least an implicit recognition that there is more than one's own sensations. Psychologists have sometimes expressed the supposed facts of mental development by saying that there is a move from concern with self to concern with non-self; that cannot be right, if only because preoccupation with one's own experiences does not entail a concern with self if no concept of the self exists. But if one starts from the supposition that the infant is initially involved with his or her own experiences and has to move from that to

78

consciousness of independent objects, there can be no adequate account of what brings about that transition. Rather one has to suppose from the start the existence of what underlies intentionality, the *in*existence of an object, as Brentano put it. But the notion of an object that is involved in that is a formal one only, so that it is not really right to suggest that consciousness of objects as such in this way necessarily involves concepts. These arise only when, as a result of learning, which is going to involve and presuppose bodily relations with the environment and with other people, apart from anything else, the formal notion of an object is given particularity, so that what one is conscious of is something seen as a such and such.

Apart from what may or may not be involved in this way in the development of an infant's consciousness and understanding, consciousness of an object in this indeterminate way is likely to be only an incidental and deviant element in normal perceptual consciousness. It may occur only, perhaps, in those cases where what is there is not, or cannot be, taken in in such a way that the object can be seen as a such and such, with the result that no sense can be made of it. Hence if one wants to speak of perception in such cases it is only because of the context of normal concept-dependent perception. If in the case of infants indeterminate consciousness of an object can exist without such a context, it would be unrealistic to speak of perception in their case, since the distinguishing features of the form of consciousness can, *ex hypothesi*, have nothing to do with the object and must therefore, if they exist, have to do simply with the characteristics of the experience (cf. n.5). It would be equally unrealistic to ask whether unconscious perception is possible in such cases. But when there is a context of normal perception, it may be that one might come to realise that one had seen something without being aware of doing so at the time, but equally without having any idea of what it was.

There is, finally, normal concept-dependent perception, when the object figures determinately for us, and is perceived as a such and such. It is such cases that I have been concerned with throughout. They are the only cases in which it is legitimate to speak of perception without qualification, and equally the only cases in which unconscious perception too can be said to occur.

Notes

1 See her (1969), 'Strategies and models of selective attention', *Psychological Review*, 76 , pp.282–99, and Neisser, Ulric (1976), *Cognition and Reality*, W.H. Freeman: San Francisco, chapter 5.

2 In my 'Perception, information and attention' in my (1983), *Perception, Learning and the Self*, Routledge and Kegan Paul: London, p.59.

3 See e.g. Weiskrantz, L. (1977), 'Trying to bridge the neuropsychological gap between monkey and man', *British Journal of Psychology*, 68, pp.431–45, and Weiskrantz and others (1974), 'Visual capacity in the hemianopic field following a restricted ablation', *Brain*, 97, pp.709–28.

4   See my (1978), *Experience and the Growth of Understanding*, Routledge and Kegan Paul: London, and some of the papers in Part 2 of my (1983), *Perception, Learning and the Self*, Routledge and Kegan Paul: London.

5   As a piece of purely anecdotal evidence, I might mention the fact that my granddaughter, Sarah, at the age of four weeks, appeared totally absorbed in the bright stripe of one of my shirts while I was holding her. I do not know what at that age she was capable of seeing at all, but the absorption was clearly a function of the brightness of something in close proximity to her. Her attention was 'grabbed'. What, if anything, was she seeing? A possible answer to that question is that, strictly speaking, she was not *seeing* anything. What she was absorbed in might have been simply the experience itself.

6   This is a point on which, in the face of some scepticism, I have insisted in various places, emphasising, as I have done at the end of chapter 3 that it is those sensations which determine the character of the total perceptual experience. I have spoken in that context of the sensations 'colouring' the perceptual experience, but I do not know if that is a helpful metaphor. See, e.g. my (1990), *In and Out of the Black Box*, Blackwell: Oxford, pp.84ff., and the references given there to chapters 1 and 4 of my *Perception, Learning and the Self*.

Chapter 11
The unity of the senses and self-consciousness

In Book 3 of his *De Anima*, having considered the individual senses, Aristotle invokes the idea of a common sense to deal with the fact that some properties of objects are perceptible via more than one sense-organ. He then goes on, as he equally does elsewhere, in the *ParvaNaturalia*, to consider other ways in which the senses may be connected or work together, e.g. we are able to discriminate between objects of different senses. To explain such facts he invokes the idea of a general form of sensibility.[1] Such a notion is close to that which Kant had in mind in speaking of the 'synthetic unity of apperception' though Kant had more general considerations in mind than the simple unity of and connection between the senses with which Aristotle was concerned. Nevertheless, the crucial point is that we cannot think of the different senses – sight, hearing and so on – as existing in independence of each other. They are each just one aspect of what perception is.

Some thinkers have appealed to what is called 'synaesthesia' in this connection. This may amount to one of two things. There is, first, the fact that the excitation of one sense-modality may produce or at least suggest ideas derived from another sense-modality. Colours may be perceived as warm or cold, and red may, as Locke said, suggest the sound of a trumpet. But such connections are really connections between the content of the experiences or ideas mediated by different modalities. They do not amount to connections between the functionings of the senses as such. There is, second, the fact that, more rarely, certain abnormal connections between parts of the brain may result in perceptions in one sense-modality producing superimposed experiences belonging to another sense-modality; the perceptions of different sounds, for example, may have associated with them experiences of different colours, which may to some extent interfere with normal vision. This, however, does not entail a real unity of hearing and vision, since the sounds simply produce visual *experiences* and these, as I have said, may well interfere with normal vision. On the other hand, what Aristotle and Kant had in mind is a real phenomenon of normal perception; there lies behind the forms of consciousness

81

provided by individual senses a more general form of consciousness, which enables us, among other things, to compare and contrast, in the course of perception, what the different senses 'tell us'. I say 'in the course of perception' because what is at issue here is not a mere intellectual survey of the functioning of the different senses. It is arguable whether Aristotle was right to think of what is involved as itself a form of sensibility or whether it is not better to side with Kant and see the form of consciousness involved as one lying behind and presupposed in sensibility. The fact remains that our experience of the world is one in which different forms of sensibility come together; the world is perceived in those terms and our conception of the world is derived from that.

It follows from all this that it is impossible to think of one sense as totally separate from others in our perception of the world. Not only is it the case, as is implied by what Aristotle says about common sensibles, that some properties of things are perceptible through more than one sense-organ, but the individual senses presuppose a more general sensibility. As I said earlier with reference to Aristotle, these are different points and raise different issues, but it would be as well to look at them in turn in more detail. As far as concerns the common sensibles it may seem obvious that one can perceive the shape of a thing, for example, by means of both sight and touch. It *is* obvious, but there is more at stake than may appear at first sight. The first question is what this fact is being contrasted with. Aristotle, for one, does not say that one cannot perceive what is *prima facie* the object of one particular sense by means of a quite different sense. He points out that, as it happens, we can sometimes tell by looking at a thing what its taste is. Of course, we should not have been able to do that unless we had learnt through experience the coincidence of that taste and that look in a given thing. Moreover, in some cases, the connection may be more than coincidence; there may be a law-like connection between one aspect of a thing, most obviously perceptible through a particular sense, and another aspect of it to which another sense may be similarly relevant. That connection too may be such that the perception of it is a function of learning, but that fact, the fact that learning is involved, is not a reason for saying (as some have done) that we should not speak of perception in such cases. It follows from all this that the fact that shape or size can be perceived via more than one sense is not to be contrasted with the supposed fact that colour, for example, is perceptible only via sight. For there is no such fact. If there were a law-like connection between the colours of things and the sounds emitted by them under certain conditions even a blind man could tell by hearing what the colour of a thing was.

Reports have sometimes been made (whether putatively genuine or not I do not know) of people who are able to tell the colours of things by passing their hands over the things in question. If such a phenomenon were a real one it might be necessary to explain it in similar terms, by positing some law-like connection between colour and some tactual property, such as temperature. To suppose otherwise would entail entering into other complications which may seem too large to resolve. The senses, as I have mentioned before but not emphasised, involve, a point of view or what is analogous to that in senses other than sight. This is a function of the kinds of causal processes which are involved. If one were to suppose that an ability to tell the colour of a thing by passing one's hands over it was a genuine visual ability and not one that depends on the kind of law-like connection between colour and a tactual property that I have mentioned, one would have to suppose the existence of something analogous to eyes in one's fingers. What would then follow would be that the point of view involved in this 'visual' perception would be one the point of origin of which would be one's fingers (for it is through them that the causal processes involved would have to be considered as taking place). As things are, our visual point of view is affected by the turning of one's eyes and head. The complications involved in the supposition that one has something like eyes in one's fingers, given out obvious ability to make quite large and variable movements of our hands, are obvious enough. A further question is whether the people in question have normal sight as well as this extra 'visual' capacity, and if so what is the relation between the two capacities and how things look by their means. If the phenomenon in question were a real one the temptation to suppose that the extra 'sense' is not a genuine visual one but one that turns on some mysterious connection between colour and some tactual property would be both immense and reasonable. The temptation to discount the reports might be even greater!

If all this seems too fanciful, one might nevertheless appeal to the fact that one can often tell from the smell of something what its taste must be. It is thus not fanciful to speak of perceiving the taste of something through smell. It is clear, however, and Aristotle points this out explicitly at *De Anima* 425a14ff., that this is not how it is with the perception of the shape of something by means of both sight and touch. One does not in that case have to learn the connection between two aspects of a thing. The aspect – shape, say – is the same in both cases. One may have to learn that that is so but not by noticing the connection between two different aspects of things. Even so, it now becomes clear that one cannot put the point simply in terms of whether a given aspect of a thing is perceptible by more than one sense. The crucial point is how that perceptibility comes about (which is perhaps why Aristotle puts the matter in terms of the availability of the aspect to different *sense-organs*, not to senses, which are simply capacities for forms of perception).

This issue has a connection with what has become known as the Molyneux problem, put forward by Molyneux in the 18th century and discussed by Locke and Berkeley, as well as by many others since. This is the question whether someone born blind who then has his or her sight restored will be able to see, without further learning, what he or she has so far perceived by touch. On the face of it, the issue is an empirical one, but one difficult to resolve, if only because a reliance on touch in making one's way round the world is likely to have an inhibitory or even distorting effect on the new use of vision. But if anything has to be learnt it is not the connection between, for example, a tactual and a visual shape, but between two different ways of picking out the same thing, the shape of the object. For it is not a matter of the coincidence in one thing of different aspects of the thing, on the basis of which the perceiver may come to be able to perceive that the thing has one such aspect on the basis of the perception via another sense-modality of another aspect of the thing. If learning enters the picture, it is rather a matter of learning that the same thing, e.g. shape, can be picked out in two different ways. A congenitally blind man whose sight is restored has to learn that what he now sees is the same thing as he has, up to now, merely felt. That is how shape looks, he may realise.

Aristotle puts the issue about the common sensibles not in terms of what is perceptible by what but in terms of the kind of relation that exists between a sense and a kind of object. In particular the question is about what kind of object is essential to the sense in question or perhaps what sense is essential to a given kind of object. The issue can be put in more modern terms by asking with respect to a given property F of an object whether that object is F if and only if it looks, sounds, ... F in normal conditions, and if so which is the sense-modality that is relevant.2 There are considerations about this into which we need not enter. The main point which requires notice here is that while it seems plausible to associate redness and sight in this way, it is not the case that something is big or curved if and *only if* looks that way in normal conditions, since one may have to bring into consideration how it feels. The best that one can say is that something is curved if and only if under normal conditions it looks, feels, or ... curved. (If one seeks a principle of unity among the appearances here, this may be a reason for speaking of a common sense, something that is a function of more than one of the sense-organs involved.) On the other hand, if the property under consideration is not simply curvature, but the more precise, geometrical, property of, say, circularity or sphericity, the exact determination of which requires measurement, no such equivalence between its incidence and the sensible appearance of the thing under normal conditions holds good. The same applies to properties of things which are in no sense at all sensory, e.g. being worth £1000.

Aristotle's account of the essential relations between a sense and a certain kind of object, e.g. between sight and colour, or its modern counterpart expressed in the sort of terms which I have indicated above, might be invoked in order to determine what a sense or sense-modality amounts to. For, as I have in effect already indicated, it is not enough simply to specify a sense by reference to the range of objects that are available to it, e.g. by saying that sight is that sense which makes colour perceptible, since those objects may be perceptible via another sense if there is a connection which makes that possible. Nor will it do to tie the sense to a given organ unless, but this makes the project trivial, the organ is determined as such by reference to the sense modality which it mediates.3 In the terms which I have suggested as following the spirit of Aristotle's original suggestion, a capacity will count as a sense if there is statable a necessary bi-conditional (a necessary 'if and only if' statement) connecting a certain kind of property of objects and a way of seeming that is made possible by that capacity. Whether that will in fact do I shall not consider further, though it is only if there is some *prima facie* way of distinguishing the senses that one can consider seriously what is involved over the question whether or not they are connected or work together. At the same time there are no conceptual considerations which can determine whether or not an organism is viable without some of the senses which are conventionally distinguished. Aristotle maintained that without touch an animal must die, though it is not clear whether this was always meant as an empirical claim or as one turning on a definition of animal life which made touch essential to such life. But while animal life certainly depends on contact with the environment, it is not obvious that such contact necessarily amounts to a sense of touch. Moreover, despite Aristotle again, no *a priori* argument can determine just how many senses there are. It remains the case that while something can, say, both look and sound noisy, that can be so for someone only if he or she has learnt that certain sorts of looks go with the production of noise. By contrast, if something both looks and feels curved no learning *of that kind* is presupposed. One may have to learn that it is curvature that presents itself in the way that it does to both sight and touch, but there is no premium in the learning process on one form of perception as against the other. Something could not look noisy to someone if he or she had no auditory experience of noise, or at any rate had no understanding of noise independent of looks, but something could certainly feel curved to people without their having any visual experience of curvature and without their having any understanding of curvature independent of feeling.

In normal perception, therefore, if one disregards the idea of a general form of sensibility, which I have yet to discuss, the senses work together only by being concerned with the same or connected objects. It is clear enough that our perception of the world must inevitably be poorer if we lack one or more senses, and, as far as deprivation of the senses is concerned, there must come a point at which perception to any real extent ceases to exist, with whatever consequences this must have for life itself. Lower organisms may have little if anything that deserves the name of perception, though they may have sense-organs which give them a primitive form of sensibility which enables them to react to their environment in ways which maintain and further life. How far up the evolutionary scale one has to come before one can speak of perception in a genuine sense is arguable. It depends on all the factors which I have discussed in previous chapters. But where one cannot speak of perception proper one cannot speak of objects of perception either, and even if there were more than one primitive form of sensibility existent in an organism there would be *a fortiori* no case for thinking of these forms of sensibility having a unity, except that they all contribute to the single biological function of the maintenance of life in the individual and in the species. To the extent that a sense is determined by the sorts of objects with which it is concerned, there is no way in which *senses* can have a unity except via those objects – and except in terms of the idea of a general form of sensibility, to which I shall now turn.

As I noted earlier, Aristotle appeals to a general form of sensibility, though not quite in such words, in noting such things as that one can discriminate between objects of different senses and that one can have what amounts to self-consciousness about the fact that one is perceiving. Aristotle does not have a concept of consciousness or at least a way in which that concept could be expressed in Greek, and he assumes that this discrimination and this self-consciousness are both forms of perception themselves, not something presupposed in and by perception.[4] By the time one comes to, say, Leibniz, one finds a distinction between perception and apperception emerging, the latter of which must be conscious. Kant argues that such apperception must constitute a unity. In the first edition of his *Critique of Pure Reason*, Kant argues for a threefold synthesis of the manifold of appearances. Experiences form a unity, first in coming together in a manifold, and second in so far as they constitute a succession in time by being held together over time (a function of memory). Finally, the manifold, united in the ways already noted, is brought in perception under a concept, which itself constitutes a principle of unity. Some of this presupposes a view of experience which, like Hume's, takes it as ultimately consisting of distinct elements, which then require unification in a way that Hume could not see as really possible. The argument might be thought to be flawed by accepting too much of the Humean view. The second edition of the *Critique* offers a much more complex argument.

It is not necessary here even to try to elucidate that argument in any detail. One might, however, concentrate on one key, and famous, remark (B131) that 'It must be possible for the 'I think' to accompany all my representations'. The phrase 'I think' is of course an echo of Descartes' *Cogito*, and it has been said, in my opinion mistakenly, that Descartes introduced a tradition of identifying consciousness with self-consciousness (as distinct, it should be pointed out, from recognising self-consciousness as one form of consciousness).[5] One might interpret the Kantian remark and its surrounding doctrine as at least saying that consciousness presupposes self-consciousness. As a thesis about every form of consciousness, including that of animals, that doctrine might be thought no less absurd than the identification of consciousness with self-consciousness. It has to be noted, however, that the use of 'my' indicates that Kant is at most talking about human beings. Moreover, and importantly, it is necessary to note that Kant says, not that the 'I think' accompanies all my representations, but that it must be possible for it to do so. If that is taken seriously, the doctrine is that consciousness presupposes self-consciousness only in the sense that in human beings for consciousness of an object (a representation) to occur it must be possible for them to be conscious of having that consciousness. If that possibility is to exist different forms of consciousness must presuppose the possibility of their being brought together under a unified consciousness, which Kant calls 'the synthetic unity of apperception'.

The senses form a unity, therefore, in that they all belong to a single self which can be conscious of itself, if only as whatever has and uses these senses, with understanding. What Kant says about the 'synthetic unity of apperception' and the possibility of self-consciousness is therefore an attempt to set out what it is for such things as senses to belong to a self (without, and this is a cardinal point of Kant's thesis, supposing that that self can be viewed as a substance of which sensibility is an attribute). In a creature in which this possibility of self-consciousness is lacking, the senses could constitute only discrete forms of sensibility; the organism in question would be capable of reacting to the world only in so far as it admits of interaction between the world and a particular sense-organ. If forms of sensibility are to be more than discrete, and so capable of more than the mediation of discrete forms of reaction to the world, they must belong to a single self; and that has no real meaning unless the self is capable of consciousness of their all belonging to it. That in turn implies the possibility of self-consciousness, a consciousness of oneself as existing over time and as related to the world in different ways, so that different aspects of that world are related in intelligible ways. When that is the case the forms of sensibility in question clearly cease to be merely discrete. I said earlier that Kant evidently had human consciousness in mind when he spoke as he did. It would be a mistake to practise *apriori* zoology here and try to draw a clear line among actual living things, so as to indicate where the conditions in question apply or fail to apply, and to do so in particular in such a way as to distinguish human beings from other living things. That the conditions apply in the case of normal human beings is clear enough. Whether any other animals satisfy the conditions is not an *apriori* matter. Nevertheless, what Kant says about the self and the possibility of self-consciousness as a condition of perception is immensely plausible. If valid, it puts limits on the range of things which we can properly be said to perceive.

Another point, which I have mentioned but which requires further emphasis, is that Kant's thesis about the 'synthetic unity of apperception' is meant to be one which connects sensibility with understanding. This is evident in what the First Edition argument says about concepts as contributing to the unity of apperception. It is evident too in the fact that in the quotation from the Second Edition argument it is the 'I think' the possibility of which can 'accompany all my representations'. The forms of consciousness and self-consciousness which Kant has in mind are not just forms of simple awareness. They are required to give intelligibility to what is brought under consciousness. Kant is right in this. For even if, as he insists, sensibility necessarily has a form which is not a matter of concepts – a temporal form and a form which is determined by spatial considerations6 – perception of the world proper requires that things are brought under concepts in such a way that things are perceived as such and suches in an intelligible way. I have emphasised both these points (that about the non-conceptual form and that about concept-use) in previous chapters. What the present chapter has to say about the way in which senses form a unity, if they do, is equally a contribution to the issue of how our understanding of the perceived world constitutes a unity, or at any rate involves a connection between different aspects of the world, in so far as they are available to perception.

Notes

1   Scholars have often taken it for granted that this general form of sensibility is the same as the common sense. I have argued against this in my (1968), *Aristotle's De Anima, Books II and III*, Clarendon Press: Oxford, and in my article (1968), 'Koine Aesthesis', *The Monist*, 52, pp.195–209. This is not the place to go into the scholarly issues about what Aristotle intended. It is clear enough, however, that the availability of certain properties of objects to more than one sense-organ is a a different issue from the fact that the workings of the senses presuppose a common sensibility which unites those senses. In the case of the common sense it is the sense-organs that are united by it, not the senses.

2   I discussed this issue in my 1964 Inaugural Lecture at Birkbeck College, 'Seeing things as they are', most of which was reprinted as an appendix to the 1969 version of my *The Psychology of Perception*, Routledge and Kegan Paul: London. For similar considerations see also Peacocke, Christopher (1983), *Sense and Content*, Clarendon Press: Oxford, chapter 2, though Peacocke spoils things in my opinion by contrasting the properties red and square (for the latter is a property the determination of which in the end requires measurement, which is not true of all 'common sensibles').

3   There are perhaps other possibilities which I shall not go into. See Grice, H.P. (1962), 'Some remarks about the senses' in Butler, R.J. (ed.), *Analytical Philosophy* (First Series), Blackwell: Oxford, Roxbee-Cox, J.W. (1970), 'Distinguishing the senses', *Mind*, 79, pp.530–50, and Heil, John (1983), *Perception and Cognition*, University of California Press: Berkeley, Los Angeles and London, chapter 1.

4   Plotinus used the term '*sunaisthesis*' in connection with the unity and mutual relationship of the senses, following Aristotle in embracing that doctrine but introducing a new term for the purpose. This has often been interpreted as signifying consciousness, and in a way it does, although the term literally means 'co-perceiving'. The Latin '*conscientia*' was used as a translation of this, although, as maintained by Stephen Toulmin in his (1982), 'The genealogy of "consciousness"' in Secord, Paul (ed.), *Explaining Human Behavior*, Sage Publications: Beverly Hills, chapter 3, the primary meaning of that term and the earliest meaning of the English 'consciousness' has to do with knowing together with others. Cudworth explicitly introduced the term 'consciousness' into philosophy as a translation of the Plotinean '*sunaisthesis*'. For Plotinus see Emilsson, E.K. (1988), *Plotinus on Sense-Perception*, C.U.P: Cambridge, p.76 and chapter 5. For Cudworth see Thiel, Udo (1994), 'Hume's notion of consciousness and reflection in context', *British Journal for the History of Philosophy*, 2, pp.75–115, esp. p.81.

5   Gadamer, Hans-Georg (1976), *Hegel's Dialectic, Five Hermeneutical Studies*, trans. with an introduction by P. Christopher Smith, Yale U.P.: New Haven and London, p.35. See also my (1986), 'Hegel on self-consciousness', *Proceedings of the British Academy*, 72, pp.317–38.

6　I put the matter in this slightly clumsy way, because, as noted in chapter 6, Kant says that representations themselves have a spatial form, and this is so only if by 'representations' is meant what sense-experiences are *of*. The confusion between sense-experiences (however described) and what they are *of* runs right through 17th and 18th century philosophy. Schopenhauer had some awareness of this, but accused Kant of insufficient idealism, rather than too much of it, insisting that there is no distinction between an experience and its object.

I began this book by raising the question what a philosophical theory of perception should consist of. In the following I have, by and large, discussed the various conditions under which perception takes place, and therefore the various components which an understanding of perception must have. I do not claim that I have discussed all that there is to this, or that I have set out all the conditions and components in question. There may well be other things that I should have mentioned, but what I have discussed is enough to justify the title of the book. Moreover, it is worth noting that some of the conditions which I have mentioned, e.g. agency and perhaps learning, have not always figured in accounts of perception. I am convinced, however, that they should be there. I have in chapter 11 discussed the sense or senses in which the senses can be conceived as forming a unity. It is important also that the various conditions of perception that I have set out should themselves not be thought of as simply discrete. It is in fact one of the dangers of discussing a concept in terms of the various conditions for its application that one may be led to think of the concept as simply the sum of those conditions. Something like that has sometimes been thought implicit in the idea of the analysis of a concept. My aim, however, has not been to provide anything that might plausibly be thought of as the analysis of the concept of perception, so that if, perhaps *per improbabile*, someone did not know what perception was he or she might learn that by adding together the various factors mentioned in spelling out the conditions of perception.

That would be implausible in any case in the present instance because I have not sought to maintain for example that whenever one perceives such and such one believes something with regard to it. Belief is not a uniform accompaniment to perception, nor have I maintained otherwise. Similar things apply to some of the other items which I have discussed under the various conditions of perception. On the other hand, it is unmistakable that perception does have a relation to belief and it is important to be clear, if possible, what that relation is. Seeing is not believing but if something could not be said to have beliefs it could not be said to perceive anything either. So in this instance a philosopher's aim might be, and indeed should be, to put perception on, so to speak, a map, on which belief is to be found also. That way of putting it has a special pertinence in connection with agency. It has seemed obvious to many philosophers (and Aristotle is especially notable in this connection) that perception involves a form of passivity. Does not one, after all, perceive when one's senses are affected? Yet Aristotle also came to see that some aspects of perception merit a description which makes 'judgment' a plausible term to use, and one of the problems which then beset him was how this 'active' aspect of perception was to be squared with what was to him, at first sight, the more obvious passivity. But there is no reason to claim that perception is something that is both active and passive, though it may well involve aspects some of which are plausibly described as passive and others which are plausibly described as active. In any case, the situation may be similar to that which I have mentioned above as applying to belief. It may be that something that could not be said to be active could not be said to perceive anything either. So perception might be related to activity without its being the case that activity is in any way a constituent of what some might call the process of perception.

Nevertheless, perception has a place on the map only if that map is of something in connection with which agency also has a place. The same applies to the other conditions which I have mentioned and discussed. On the other hand, more is to be said of some of those conditions. Perception, I have insisted, is concept-dependent; it presupposes a relation of intentionality to something which constitutes at least an intentional object; and, at any rate when that intentionality involves consciousness, the consciousness has the form that it has because it is mediated by a particular kind of experience which is the product of causal processes involving a particular sense-organ and all that makes that functional. As I said a little earlier, it would be a mistake to suppose that in listing those conditions one is providing an analysis of the concept of perception. That would be to omit all the other conditions – imagination, learning, the possibility of self-consciousness, as well as those which I have already mentioned – a reference to which is essential to an understanding of perception but are not such that all instances of perception involve them directly. Hence, even if it is the case that all perception involves concepts and intentionality subject to the satisfaction of particular causal conditions, it would certainly not be enough to mention these things in order to make clear what perception is. Nor can one simply add in characteristic forms of experience, even if they are generally present, and even if one needs reference to characteristic forms of experience in order to make clear what intentionality amounts to in this instance. For, not all perception is conscious, and where it is not, there cannot be conscious forms of experience either. Does one want to insist that there are present forms of experience all the same?

There may be cases in which one *would* want to insist on that, but it might be better to rely on the presumption of a context of conscious perception. even if consciousness is lacking in the particular case in question. The satisfaction of the conditions of intentionality, concept-use, and subjection to particular causal processes is necessary if perception is to occur, because perception must have an object, that object must be brought under concepts which give it intelligibility, and this is not simply a function of thought; it is brought about by things that happen to and in the body in its relations to the world of which it is a part. That summary has some similarity to what Reid said about perception – that while it might be 'suggested' by sensation it also involved a conception of an object, and a belief in its existence which is immediate and not the result of reasoning. I have given reason to dispute the point about belief, at any rate as Reid makes it, but the other points seem right. The point about the belief being immediate requires qualification if belief is not necessary, but it remains true that the relation to an object and what it is conceived as is not a product of thought alone and is not mediated by thought or inference. A reference to the part played by certain causal processes may help to take care of that point and its implications.

I would insist again, however, that saying the sort of thing that Reid says is not enough to make clear what perception is, even if he was right in trying to combat contemporary views of the matter which tended to assimilate perception to a kind of sensation. I do not know if someone who went through the kind of discussion of the subject which I have provided would be likely to say 'Yes, now I know what perception is.' I for one would be unhappy if they did. For, if my metaphor of a map is sound, it is not the function of a map to tell one exactly what the terrain mapped is like. It will do something to that end and will, if interpreted rightly, provide a guide for one concerned to make a way through the terrain or to draw some conclusions about the practicality of that. But a map is not a detailed picture or description of what is mapped. Conclusions such as those which might be derived from a map might also be drawn from the kind of discussions on which I have been engaged, although the practicality in question will be one having to do with intellectual possibilities. I believe that what I have said has some morals for cognitive psychology and cognitive science, but I shall not repeat in that connection the kind of thing I have said elsewhere.[1]

However that may be, what I have said here is certainly meant to be a contribution to a theory of perception in the philosophical sense, and is to be judged on that basis. One other point perhaps needs to be made. My discussion contains a fair amount of history of philosophy. The justification for that lies partly in the consideration that it is a good thing to express approval of one's predecessors when they have said things that seem right or nearly right. But in any case a philosophical theory of perception (and indeed of anything else), as a conceptual exercise, cannot stand by itself without any relation to the conceptions of the things that fall within its domain that have been put forward by great minds concerned with it. A philosophical theory cannot remain in a historical vacuum, so to speak. The other metaphor which I have employed, that of a map, fails at this point. A map of a terrain is not necessarily improved by making clear its relation to previous maps. For a terrain is a terrain, however much it may change. But a conceptual map, if it can be called that, is concerned with the best way of expressing what is involved in thinking about a certain matter. That requires consideration both of the thinking and of its expression. That is likely to be more illuminating if it is related to some extent to what has been done in that way in the past. A philosophical theory is to that extent unlike other kinds of theory.

So what is perception? No straight answer to that is likely to be profitable. But an account of its conditions may help the understanding. That is what a philosophical theory should be expected to do.

Note

1   Particularly in my (1990), *In and Out of the Black Box*, Blackwell: Oxford.